TUDOR
GOVERNMENT

QUESTIONS AND ANALYSIS IN HISTORY

Edited by Stephen J. Lee and Sean Lang

Other titles in this series:

Imperial Germany, 1871–1918
Stephen J. Lee

The Weimar Republic
Stephen J. Lee

Hitler and Nazi Germany
Stephen J. Lee

Parliamentary Reform, 1785–1928
Sean Lang

The French Revolution
Jocelyn Hunt

The Spanish Civil War
Andrew Forrest

The English Wars and Republic, 1637–1660
Graham E. Seel

The Renaissance
Jocelyn Hunt

The Cold War
Bradley Lightbody

Stalin and the Soviet Union
Stephen J. Lee

TUDOR GOVERNMENT

T. A. MORRIS

ROUTLEDGE

London and New York

First published 1999
by Routledge
11 New Fetter Lane, London EC4P 4EE

Simultaneously published in the USA and Canada
by Routledge
29 West 35th Street, New York, NY 10001

Routledge is an imprint of the Taylor & Francis Group

Typeset in Grotesque and Perpetua by Keystroke, Jacaranda Lodge,
Wolverhampton
Printed and bound in Great Britain by Clays Ltd, St Ives plc

British Library Cataloguing in Publication Data
A catalogue record for this book is available from the British Library

Library of Congress Cataloging in Publication Data
Morris, T. A. (Terence Alan), 1949–
    Tudor government / T.A. Morris.
      p.   cm. (Questions and analysis in history)
    Includes bibliographical references and index.
      1. Great Britain––Politics and government––1485–1603––
Handbooks, manuals, etc. 2. Tudor, House of––Handbooks,
manuals, etc. I. Title. II. Series.
DA315.M63   1999
320.442'09'031––dc21   98–33199
                                              CIP

ISBN 0–415–19149–1

CONTENTS

Series preface   vii
Acknowledgements   viii

1   The personal element in Tudor monarchy   1

2   Court and patronage   20

3   The central organs and offices of government   38

4   Central government: law and order   54

5   The government of the localities   72

6   The role of Parliament   92

7   Government of the Church   109

8   Finance   128

    Notes and sources   145
    Select bibliography   157
    Index   159

SERIES PREFACE

Most history textbooks now aim to provide the student with interpretation, and many also cover the historiography of a topic. Some include a selection of sources.

So far, however, there have been few attempts to combine *all* the skills needed by the history student. Interpretation is usually found within an overall narrative framework and it is often difficult to separate out the two for essay purposes. Where sources are included, there is rarely any guidance as to how to answer the questions on them.

The Questions and Analysis series is therefore based on the belief that another approach should be added to those which already exist. It has two main aims.

The first is to separate narrative from interpretation so that the latter is no longer diluted by the former. Most chapters start with a background narrative section containing essential information. This material is then used in a section focusing on analysis through a specific question. The main purpose of this is to help to tighten up essay technique.

The second aim is to provide a comprehensive range of sources for each of the issues covered. The questions are of the type which appear on examination papers, and some have worked answers to demonstrate the techniques required.

The chapters may be approached in different ways. The background narratives can be read first to provide an overall perspective, followed by the analyses and then the sources. The alternative method is to work through all the components of each chapter before going on to the next.

ACKNOWLEDGEMENTS

Author and publisher are grateful to the following for permission to reproduce copyright material.

I. Arthurson: *Documents of the Reign of Henry VII* (University of Cambridge Local Examinations Syndicate 1984). G. Cavendish: *The Life of Cardinal Wolsey* (George Routledge 1890). C. Cross: *The Royal Supremacy in the Elizabethan Church* (George Allen and Unwin 1969). G.R. Elton: *The Tudor Constitution* (University of Cambridge Press 1965). T.E. Hartley (ed.): *Proceedings in the Parliaments of Elizabeth I. Vol. I. 1558–1581* (University of Leicester 1981). J. Hurstfield and A.G.R. Smith: *Elizabethan People: State and Society* (Arnold 1977). M. Levine: *Tudor Dynastic Problems* (George Allen and Unwin 1973). S. Newman: *Reading Historical Documents. Yorkists and Tudors* (Blackwell 1989). D. O'Sullivan and R. Lockyer: *Longman Sources and Opinions. Tudor England* (Longman 1993). A.F. Pollard: *The Reign of Henry VII from Contemporary Sources. Vol. III* (Longman 1914). G.W. Prothero: *Statutes and Constitutional Documents, 1558–1625.* (Oxford University Press 1913). G. Regan: *Elizabeth I* (University of Cambridge Press 1988). J.R. Tanner: *Tudor Constitutional Documents* (Cambridge 1951). C.H. Williams (ed.): *English Historical Documents 1485–1558* (Eyre and Spottiswoode 1967).

1

THE PERSONAL ELEMENT IN TUDOR MONARCHY

BACKGROUND NARRATIVE

England, like most of Western Europe, was ruled by a monarchy and had been for some six centuries before the Tudors occupied the throne. In that time a range of principles had been developed to justify and to support royal government. Like their continental counterparts, English kings claimed that they ruled by divine right, by the will of God, and that they were therefore the guarantors of the stability and order that God desired on earth. In pre-Reformation Europe, such a claim facilitated a fruitful working partnership with the Church. Rebellion against the monarch was generally equated with rebellion against God and, if the rebels were defeated, they could expect to suffer horrible punishments that reflected the appalling nature of the crime of treason. If they won, and both Henry VII and Mary came to the throne essentially as successful rebels, then their triumph was represented as illustrating the divine will. The English crown passed from one generation to another by the principle of primogeniture, the right of the eldest surviving son to succeed the father. English monarchs, like others across Europe, went to considerable lengths to avoid the succession of a woman, generally considered to be incapable of exercising the coercive functions that lay at the heart of monarchy. While they did not follow France in instituting a Salic Law, which formally forbade the succession of a female, they much preferred the succession of a younger prince to that of an older princess. Thus, in 1547, the nine-year-old Edward VI succeeded his father, despite the fact that he had two half-sisters older than him. If fate forced a female ruler upon them, most people assumed that, like Mary Tudor, she would marry a strong husband, who would be capable of controlling the realm for her.

At the beginning of the Tudor era the king was still in large part a warlord. It remained his primary duty to conduct the defence of the realm, to resist encroachments upon the territories and rights of his dynasty, and to combat domestic disorder. It remained true in the reigns of the first two Tudors that the king was expected to carry out such duties in person, at the head of his armies, and it required extensive rethinking to accommodate monarchs who, on account of their youth or their gender, could not fulfil these expectations. The monarch was also the protector and enforcer of the laws of the kingdom. The crown held a highly privileged position within the legal structure of the realm, but was expected to act within that structure. The powers of the Tudor monarchs were extensive, yet clearly limited. A range of political and economic functions was exclusively reserved for the monarch and none other: these constituted the royal 'prerogative'. The monarch alone could declare war and conclude peace, arrange the marriages of members of the royal family, pardon offenders, summon and dissolve Parliament, or manage the coinage. In other respects the monarch was bound by the law. Even so strong-willed a ruler as Henry VIII felt the need to give legal basis to his break from Rome, and despite her strong conviction that her father's actions had been contrary to the will of God, Queen Mary could not reverse them without due process of statute law.

This was one of several respects in which Tudor monarchy was based upon a fine balance of compromise and cooperation. Unable to levy taxes at will, and with an income largely dependent upon customs duties and rents from crown lands, the monarch could afford neither a standing army nor a large bureaucracy with which to control the localities. Effective royal government, therefore, depended upon an effective working partnership with the greatest and the wealthiest of the crown's subjects. Such a partnership can be seen in operation throughout the sixteenth century in the political life of the Court (see Chapter 2), and on occasion in Parliament (see Chapter 6). It was increasingly claimed by sixteenth-century constitutional theorists that the authority of the crown was enhanced by the acknowledgement of the major 'estates of the realm', the Church, the nobility and the representatives of the major towns. The monarch was never more powerful than when he or she sat in Parliament, surrounded by members of those estates.

It was equally important that the monarch should maintain the dominant position in this partnership. It was one of the peculiarities of Henry VII's reign that he sought to control the nobility and other leading subjects by fear. Thereafter, the monarch assumed the more traditional role of the 'fount of honour', winning personal loyalty, and rewarding faithful service with titles, lands and riches, to ensure that local influence and prestige were exercised in the interests of the Tudor monarchy. It was one of the major factors in the success of the Tudor dynasty that, by one means or another, the King or Queen succeeded in maintaining the upper hand. This was all the more remarkable in that for nearly sixty years of the Tudor era England had no adult male monarch. Henry VIII's death brought a minor to the throne, with all the practical and theoretical problems of a protectorate, and Edward VI's own premature death (1553) raised even more complex difficulties. Not only was England ruled by women for the next fifty years, but by women who had at one stage or another been declared illegitimate and been specifically barred from the succession. It is hard to determine whether Mary's decision to marry a foreign prince caused greater political difficulties and tensions than Elizabeth's decision not to marry at all, and to exercise the crown's authority in her own right. Had Elizabeth died from the attack of smallpox that she suffered in 1563, her experiment would have been written off as an aberration, and possibly as a disastrous one. In the event, in G.R. Elton's words, 'Elizabeth's long life postponed the crisis until it had ceased to be one,' and gave the Queen and those about her the opportunity to develop unprecedented justifications for a female monarchy.

We must not forget that, fifty years into the Tudor era, the nature of their monarchy changed dramatically. The Act of Supremacy (1534) established by statute law that, quite apart from his political authority, Henry VIII was also supreme head of the Church in England. A flurry of other acts transferred to him the powers over ecclesiastical law, church appointments and church revenue that had hitherto been vested in the papacy. A new Treason Law (1534) made it as serious an offence to deny this ecclesiastical authority as it was to deny any of the crown's more traditional, political powers. However much English theorists might claim that these powers had traditionally belonged to the crown, and been usurped by Rome in recent centuries, these changes must be seen as the most fundamental in the history of the English monarchy. Although this Royal Supremacy has survived until the present day, it encountered some serious obstacles in the latter part of the sixteenth century. The accession of Edward VI raised the issue of whether the Supremacy could be exercised by a mere boy, while that of Elizabeth posed the tougher problem of whether a woman, barred from all other positions of ecclesiastical authority, could exercise the highest authority of all. In between, of course, Mary Tudor opted to return to the Roman Church, and rejected the Supremacy outright.

ANALYSIS (1): HOW IMPORTANT, AND HOW SUCCESSFUL, WAS THE ELEMENT OF FEAR IN THE ESTABLISHMENT OF ROYAL AUTHORITY UNDER HENRY VII?

Historians have traditionally regarded the reign of Henry VII as a success. After a number of short or disrupted reigns the first Tudor established his own power for nearly twenty-five years, and handed it on to a dynasty that retained it for nearly a century. Much work on Henry VII, therefore, has been primarily concerned to establish the secret of his success. For very many years the widely accepted interpretation was that supplied by J.R. Green. (1) The last decades of the fifteenth century, he asserted, had witnessed the establishment of a 'New Monarchy', which had as its distinctive features financial solvency and centralised institutions of government directed by an autocratic monarch, and which was staffed by 'middle-class' administrators who thus reduced the political influence of the feudal nobility.

Much later work on the early Tudors modified the detail, but not the central suppositions of Green's argument. While F.C. Dietz (2) outlined the consolidation of crown finances and highlighted the achievement of solvency, K.W. Pickthorn (3) and G.R. Elton (4) examined the development of political and financial institutions. The success of Henry VII's reign appeared to be based upon his ability to substitute stable government for civil disorder, often through the more effective operation of traditional institutions, and upon the personal industry and application that the King brought to these tasks. Francis Bacon's portrait of a workaholic monarch stood the test of time very well indeed: 'He did by pleasures as great princes do by banquets, come and look a little upon them and then turn away. For never prince was more wholly given to his affairs.' More recent writers, however, have begun to criticise this approach, as ignoring the personal and factional elements that lay at the very roots of political life. The study of Tudor monarchy has begun to focus upon the practical means by which Henry won respect for his person and for his authority. This process in turn has highlighted the means by which he inspired fear among those whose hostility, or apathy, might have been dangerous for him.

Henry invented few new weapons for the enforcement of his authority, but used established methods in a distinctive and intensive way. The number of attainders (5) passed during his reign was remarkably similar to the number passed by Edward IV: 138 and 140, respectively. Yet, while Edward used them predominantly in the early, unstable years of his reign, they were a consistent feature of Henry's Parliaments. Only that of 1497 produced no acts of attainder while, to compensate, 51 were passed in the Parliament of 1504 alone. His use of bonds and recognisances (6) was equally intensive and far-reaching. Their application was particularly severe in the first decade of the sixteenth century, at which stage, as J.R. Lander (7) has claimed, 'the list of nobles under bonds and recognisances, either for their own good behaviour or that of others, reads almost like a role-call of the English peerage.' Of 62 noble families, 46 or 47 were at this time 'in the King's danger' in one form or another. The primary purpose of such tactics remains in some doubt, for it is by no means clear that Henry made very great financial gains from them. Lord Burgavenny appears to have paid only about a thousand pounds of the enormous seventy-thousand-pound fine slapped on him in 1507 for illegal retaining, and this convinces many historians that the King's primary motive was fear rather than financial gain. 'Henry's aim', as Lander has defined it, 'seems to have been to keep his nobility (and other people) in subjection through legal terrorisation and the dread of financial ruin.'

Once forced to accept that Henry employed unsavoury methods, historians have produced a number of mitigating explanations. Some have seen it as a necessary evil, claiming, like Roger Lockyer (8), that 'failure to act effectively would have meant a return to anarchy'. G.R. Elton (9), similarly, believed that the times justified the solutions that Henry adopted, that 'he governed well and wisely by methods which those who evaded the law might well resent but which represented no rapacity and required no remorse'. Yet several authorities have questioned whether such methods really were necessary, and whether the English nobility really had the desire or the capacity at this time to mount a serious challenge to the King's authority. J.A.F. Thomson (10) has stressed the damage done to the great feudal families by the recent political upheavals, leaving the Staffords, the Howards and, by 1489, the Percies with minors at their head. Lander has shown that the political behaviour of the nobility was relatively good, that only a handful of English lords were involved in the rebellions of Henry's reign, and that the so-called 'Yorkist opposition' consisted mainly of 'Irish lords and a few ambitious and disgruntled relations' of the former monarchs. Alternatively, historians have portrayed a wise and effective monarch whose judgement deteriorated in the years after 1502 under the pressures of bereavement and declining health. S.B. Chrimes (11) has noted that the personal and political pressures that resulted from the deaths of Prince Arthur (1502) and Queen Elizabeth of York (1503) 'left him a very lonely and much aged man, with no one close enough and old enough to fill the gaps in his domestic circle'. A third approach has been to view such measures as a pragmatic response to the enormous practical difficulties that Henry faced in the local enforcement of his authority. Professor Chrimes has noted how little concern he demonstrated for formal law enforcement, and that 'there is little evidence that any very striking attempts were made to enforce it, except where it redounded to the financial interest of the crown'. Lander extends this argument with the suggestion that formal enforcement was so notoriously difficult, especially in the distant localities, that Henry resorted to alternative means: 'Rather than dealing out impartial justice, Henry indulged in arbitrary terrorisation and financial extortion against selected victims, both high and low.' He chose 'to pounce upon selected individuals in a cat-and-mouse manner,' rather than prosecute them through the normal channels. Even Star Chamber, traditionally the epitome of personalised legal enforcement by the crown, saw very few prosecutions for maintenance in Henry's reign, and even fewer that resulted in the punishment of the accused.

Only very recently have some writers come to view the use of such tactics as evidence of fundamental weaknesses in Henry's kingship. J.R. Lander concluded some years ago that Henry's mistrust of his more powerful subjects arose from his inexperience and from the peculiarity of his position in 1485. 'He was an exile, a stranger to the English scene, with no experience in government or in administration of any kind. Henry was well aware of the fact that he had managed to seize the country with very little force at his command, and that if one man could so easily overthrow a government so probably could another.' Under such circumstances, the nobility did not need to show hostility, for their caution and reserve appeared sufficiently dangerous in themselves. Christine Carpenter (12) has gone further than this, interpreting Henry's tactics as evidence of a fundamental failure to govern according to the norms of late medieval kingship. In Carpenter's view Henry VII, with his total inexperience of English politics, failed to understand, and thus failed to exploit, those relationships with the feudal nobility by which his predecessors governed, and by which they gained control of the localities. The same author's research into local political relationships in Warwickshire, Derbyshire and Staffordshire has confirmed the extent to which the crown bypassed local power structures and relied instead upon the loyalty of bureaucrats such as Bray, Belknap, Empson and Dudley. The final element in Carpenter's critique of Henry's kingship is her assertion that his tactics failed. Rather than ensuring stability, they ensured that 'he remained throughout his reign a usurper, buying the loyalty of his closest servants, forcing that of his subjects at large'. The real secret of the Tudors' success was not Henry VII's firm rule in the early 1500s, so much as his son's shrewdness, in 1509, in rejecting those policies and destroying some of his father's leading agents. It might be noted that Henry VIII cancelled 45 recognisances in the first year of his reign, 130 over the next five years, and explicitly condemned 55 of them as illegal. The tactics of the first Tudor kept him on the throne, but did little to create the political stability that was normally a priority for his successors. The continued danger of rebellion up to 1497, the instability generated by Prince Arthur's death in 1502, and the draconian punishment of Lord Burgavenny in 1507 all help to create a sense of continuing crisis, which is no longer evident in the early years of Henry VIII's reign.

While agreeing that Henry found himself in an unusually difficult position in 1485, Margaret Condon (13) takes a more sympathetic view of his response, discerning in it a degree of political logic. Having no extensive and reliable royal kin through which to govern, and lacking the financial means to create an extensive nobility loyal to himself, Henry found himself saddled with a nobility that he had no positive reason to trust. Assuming that they might accept another pretender as meekly as they had accepted him, he exploited existing means of exerting pressure to protect a position far more vulnerable than historians have usually been prepared to admit. It may be that Henry's success as a ruler should not be sought in constitutional theories of monarchy or in institutional development, but in the intense and ruthless pragmatism that a late medieval monarch needed to use. Benjamin Thompson (14) is probably perfectly accurate in his judgement that 'in Henry's own eyes, keeping the throne and handing it on to his heirs was probably the fundamental priority, far more important than the quality of the rule he offered'.

Questions

1. 'Henry VII did far more to establish his personal authority than to re-establish the institutional stability of the English crown.' To what extent do you agree with this statement?
2. In what respects was the English monarchy stronger at the time of Henry VII's death than it had been in 1485?

ANALYSIS (2): DID EITHER SOMERSET OR NORTHUMBERLAND (15) SUCCEED IN SOLVING THE PROBLEMS OF EFFECTIVE ROYAL GOVERNMENT AT A TIME OF ROYAL MINORITY?

The personal, royal authority established by Henry VII and Henry VIII was put to the test in January 1547, when the King's death brought to the throne a nine-year-old boy, manifestly unable to enforce his political will through the strength of his own personality. Historical interpretations of the reign of Edward VI have been heavily influenced by contemporary fears that the realm would revert to feudal rivalries and to chronic instability. Many writers have seen this as a period in which stable royal government really was in severe danger of disintegration, with Dale Hoak (16) concluding that 'in October 1549 the machinery of royal government actually broke down'. Similarly, the traditionally hostile interpretation of the Duke of Northumberland's administration has led many to share W.G. Hoskins' (17) unequivocal conclusion that after 1549 the realm was in the hands of 'the most unprincipled gang of political adventurers and predators that England had seen for many centuries'.

In his will Henry VIII envisaged the maintenance of royal government by a Council of Regency that would collectively exercise the young King's authority until such time as he could do so personally. One of the first acts of that Council, however, was to appoint Edward Seymour, the King's uncle, to the office of Lord Protector. In doing so the councillors were exercising the authority that Henry had vested in them for the better running of the realm, yet they were acting on what proved to be old-fashioned principles. The original idea of the protectorate was to provide leadership for the Regency Council, and Somerset's claims to exercise such leadership were based upon the traditional strengths of a blood relationship with the King and a formidable military reputation. Somerset evidently failed to grasp this, and quickly moved to give himself greater independent and personal authority. In the course of 1547 he threw off the obligation to abide by the Council's advice, gained the authority to appoint anyone of his choice to the Council, and finally established his complete independence from any obligation to consult the Council at all. For the only time in the sixteenth century a large proportion of the royal powers passed into the hands of a subject. A.F. Pollard (18) concluded that Somerset had 'seized unfettered the royal power of the Tudors', and Dale Hoak claims similarly that 'effectively Somerset was King: he could order action under the King's signature at his own convenience'.

For all his powers, few historians would now dispute that Somerset's protectorate was a failure, ending in the breakdown of his relations with other ministers and councillors, who forced him from office in October 1549. For many years this failure was blamed upon Somerset's enemies, for in Pollard's influential interpretation, he suffered for the enlightenment of his social and religious views. Tolerant in his attitudes to religion and towards contemporary social problems, he was ousted by colleagues whose conventional self-interest made them intolerant of such 'advanced' thinking. Such an interpretation was eventually challenged by Michael Bush (19), who portrayed the Protector as a much more conventional Tudor politician, substantially preoccupied with the war against Scotland, upon which his military reputation rested. Bush argued that he pursued 'tolerant' policies in other respects because he lacked the financial and military resources to do otherwise, and that his fall resulted primarily from the failure of his Scottish policies and his perceived responsibility for the severe social unrest that shook the realm in 1549. Dale Hoak adjusted this argument by emphasising Somerset's political methods, rather than his policies. His work on the register of Council business revealed that by 1549 Somerset had 'virtually ceased to work with the Council and increasingly dispatched the King's business through the officers and channels of his own household'. Examining the problem from the angle of the Court rather than that of the Council, John Murphy (20) has added that, in addition to offending the leading politicians of the realm in this way, the Protector was clumsy in his handling of the King himself, and that 'government by a protector from his own household had none of the legitimacy of the Privy Chamber politics of Henry VIII's last years'. Summing up this argument, David Loades (21) concludes that Somerset fell 'because he lacked that instinctive grasp of the possible which is essential in all effective leaders'. Preoccupied with his theoretical powers as Protector, and perhaps with his status as the

King's uncle, he failed to appreciate that it was impossible to exercise royal authority without sufficient claim to it, or to govern without due consultation with the leading political figures of the realm.

Somerset's successor at the head of the King's government has had a bad press. The traditional portrayal of the Duke of Northumberland is of a man who usurped royal power, engineered Somerset's death, put his friends and supporters into positions of power and finally, as the King lay dying, sponsored a blatant usurpation of the throne. Here is the archetype of the 'overmighty subject' and the lowest ebb of Tudor monarchy. Yet, between 1549 and the crisis of Edward's last illness, Northumberland governed very largely through orthodox channels, and largely in conformity with Henry VIII's will. He worked as Lord President of the Council, rather than taking his predecessor's discredited title, and Hoak accepts that 'it was the Duke's very deliberate aim to restore the Council's recognised competence. It was his achievement to reestablish the Privy Council as the King's chief instrument of government.' Admittedly, he staffed the Council with his own supporters, and placed others in the royal household to ensure his influence with the King. In particular, historians have commented upon the roles played there by Sir Thomas Darcy as Captain of the Guard and by Sir John Gates, who controlled the dry stamp of Edward's signature. Yet this need not appear particularly sinister. Given the fate that overtook Somerset, and which had overtaken Northumberland's own father, Edmund Dudley, it would have been strange if he had not taken precautions to limit the influence of his enemies. John Murphy has argued that there was little more in these measures than political common sense, and that Northumberland's baser motives have not been proven: 'It would have been a foolish councillor who would have forced upon his sovereign personal servants whom he was bound to dislike. The new personnel in the Privy Chamber shared two characteristics: the King's religion and the King's personal favour.' In short, it is becoming less convincing to view Northumberland as a 'political pirate', eager to plunder the legitimate authority of the crown for his own gain. Historians are increasingly inclined to support David Loades's view that the Lord President's manoeuvres 'were directed, not to seizing the crown, but to establishing himself as the guide and mentor of a new and formidable Tudor king'. Whatever their ultimate motive, his tactics emphasised the positions of the King and his Council at the centre of government, and illustrated his awareness that he could only rule through orthodox and well-established royal channels.

The main obstacle to Northumberland's rehabilitation is the fact that, as the King's health deteriorated rapidly in the summer of 1553, he played a leading role in the attempt to exclude Mary Tudor from the succession. The terms of Henry's last Act of Succession were ultimately set aside in favour of Lady Jane Grey, and the fact that 'Queen Jane' had recently been married to Northumberland's son has suggested that he was the prime mover in this conspiracy. The crucial factor in this crisis, and in any wider assessment of Edward's reign, is the political and intellectual development of the young King. Yet it remains extremely difficult to estimate the degree of political involvement and influence that he enjoyed in the latter stages of his short life. Dale Hoak, despite his largely positive interpretation of Northumberland's policies, was convinced that Edward's increasingly frequent participation in Council meetings was carefully prepared and orchestrated by Northumberland. The King was at best 'a student merely following the course of state business, not directing it'. W.K. Jordan's (22) view, however, was that Edward at this juncture genuinely stood 'on the threshold of power', and his interpretation has received support from David Loades and Penry Williams (23). Working from the political chronicle kept by the King from 1550, they have found ample evidence of his growing political maturity. Even if Edward was not in control of government on the eve of his death, they conclude, he was being prepared systematically for such control. These writers conclude that the central factor in the 1553 crisis was Edward's own determination to prevent a Catholic succession. Indeed, Dale Hoak himself agrees that 'barring Mary from the succession was a cause in which the young King believed'. If Edward did indeed take the initiative in this matter, he was exercising the royal will in a manner worthy of his father. In the view of Professor Loades, 'Edward attempted to flout the standing legislation on the subject [of the succession] and deny the competence of statute via a deliberate exercise of despotic will.' According to the traditional view, once Edward was dead, Northumberland simply bullied the Council into compliance with him. It is probably more useful to see the councillors faced at this moment with an extraordinarily difficult constitutional decision. Faced with the direct orders of their King, and the claims of his half-sister, well founded in statute law, they wavered and briefly accepted the proclamation of 'Queen Jane', before abandoning Northumberland and making their own peace with Queen Mary (see Chapter 3). Perhaps the Lord President himself was caught in this trap for, as B.L. Beer (24) has pointed out, the accession of Mary 'did not necessarily mean his ruin. The safest course would have been to make peace with Mary.' From this angle, it was not Northumberland's actions that made him a traitor, but the subsequent fact of Mary's success. Far from illustrating the subversion of royal authority by an 'overmighty subject', this interpretation of events suggests a considerable degree of personal toughness on Edward's part, as well as on the part of Mary, together with a highly developed respect on the part of the councillors for legitimate royal authority.

It may appear that the remarkable thing about the reign of Edward VI is not that it illustrates the weaknesses of monarchy in the hands of a minor, but that it shows how, even with a minor on the throne, contemporary politicians felt deeply constrained by the rules and the mystique of monarchy. Somerset and Northumberland failed and died because, even with a considerable degree of practical power in their hands, one tried to exercise a direct, royal authority to which he had no claim, while the other, after governing successfully 'by the rules' for some time, was left high and dry by the death of the young monarch on whose support and whose real authority he depended.

Questions

1. Was the authority of the English monarchy seriously at risk during the minority of Edward VI?
2. What arguments are there for claiming that Northumberland conducted the government of the realm more responsibly than Somerset had done?

SOURCES

1. HENRY VII'S USE OF BONDS AND RECOGNISANCES

Source A: from Polydore Vergil's *Anglica Historia*, published in 1534.

Henry, after he had subdued the final conspiracy against him and established peaceful relations with all neighbouring kings, might now after many anxieties and dangers relax his mind in peace, but he became at once preoccupied with a fresh care. For he began to treat his subjects with more harshness and severity than had been his custom in order (as he himself asserted) to ensure that they remained more thoroughly and entirely in obedience to him. The people themselves had another explanation for his action, for they considered that they were suffering not on account of their own sins but on account of the greed of their monarch. All of his subjects who were men of substance, when found guilty of whatever fault, he harshly fined in order to make the population less well able to undertake any upheaval and to discourage at the same time all offences.

Source B: from Francis Bacon's *History of the Reign of Henry VII*, published in 1622.

And with his justice, he was also a merciful prince: as in whose time there were but three of the nobility that suffered; the Earl of Warwick, the Lord Chamberlain, and the Lord Audley. But the less blood he drew, the more he took of treasure. This excess of his had at that time many glosses and interpretations. Some thought the continual rebellions, wherewith he had been vexed, had made him grow to hate his people; some thought it was done to pull down their stomachs [pride], and to keep them low; some, for that he would leave his son a golden fleece; some suspected he had some high design upon foreign parts. But those perhaps shall come nearest the truth that fetch not their reasons so far off, but rather impute it to nature, age, peace, and a mind fixed upon no other ambition or pursuit. Whereunto I should add, that having every day occasion to take notice of the necessities and shifts for money of other great princes abroad, it did the better, by comparison, set off to him the felicity of full coffers.

Source C: part of the recognisance made between the King and Lord Burgavenny in December 1507.

Indenture between the King and George, Lord Burgavenny; whereas George is indebted to the King in [the sum of] one hundred thousand pounds or thereabouts for unlawful retaining, done in Kent, contrary to certain laws and statutes; and whereas the King may keep him in prison and take all his lands until the whole sum be paid; the King is graciously contented to accept as parcel [part payment] of the debt the sum of five thousand pounds, payable over ten years, for which payments George binds himself and his heirs.

Source D: from the confession and petition of Edmund Dudley, composed in the Tower of London before his execution, 1509.

And also the pleasure and mind of the king's grace, whose soul God pardon, was much set to have many persons in his danger at his pleasure, and that as well spiritual men as temporal men.

[There follows a list of thirty-one cases, including the following:]

Item one obligation of my lord [bishop] of London for 500 pounds, and a recognisance of 300 pounds to be paid at certain days: he was hardly dealt withal herein, for he said unto me by his priesthood the matter laid against him was not true.

Item the abbot of Furness had a hard end for his pardon for he paid and is deemed to pay 500 marks for a little matter.

Item one Hawkyns of London, draper, upon the surmise of a lewd fellow, paid 100 marks for a light matter.

Item the king's grace had of one Hubbard for the office of weighing of wools at Southampton 50 marks, which Hubbard never had the office, but one Troyes had it.

Item the earl of Northumberland was bound to the king in many great sums, howbeit the king's mind was to have payment of two thousand pounds and no more, as his grace showed me, yet that was too much for ought that was known.

Item one Haslewood was kept long in prison and paid a great sum of money upon a light ground.

Item the Bishop of Salisbury paid 1000 marks for a very light cause.

Source E: from a report made to the Duke of Milan, July 1496.

I asked him (a Florentine who had been in England for some time) about English affairs. He said that the King is rather feared than loved, and this was due to his avarice. I asked who ruled him and had control over him. He said there was only Master Bray, who controls the King's treasure. The King is very powerful in money, but if fortune allowed some lord of the blood royal to rise, and he had to take the field, he would fare badly owing to his avarice; the people would abandon him; they would treat him as they did King Richard.

Source F: from the eulogy delivered by Sir Thomas More upon the coronation of Henry VIII, 1509.

Now the people, liberated, run before their king with bright faces. Now the nobility, long since at the mercy of the dregs of the population, lifts its head and rejoices in such a king – and with good reason. Now the merchant, previously deterred by numerous taxes, once again ploughs seas grown unfamiliar. Now laws, previously powerless, or even bent to unjust ends, have happily regained their proper force. No longer is it a criminal offence to own honestly acquired property. No longer does fear hiss whispered secrets in one's ear.

Questions

1. Explain the following references that appear in these sources: 'the Earl of Warwick' (Source B); 'unlawful retaining . . . contrary to certain laws and statutes' (Source C); 'they would treat him as they did King Richard' (Source E).
2. Compare the explanations given by Polydore Vergil (source A) and by Francis Bacon (Source B) of Henry's behaviour in the latter years of his reign.

*3. To what extent do Sources C and D support the contention that the harshness of Henry's rule was motivated by 'avarice'?

4. To what extent do these sources, and any other evidence known to you, support the claim that 'although the governmental methods employed by Henry VII were widely unpopular, they were also highly successful'?

Worked answer

*3. [This question must be answered strictly with reference to these two nominated sources. In addition to detecting evidence of Henry's 'avarice', or greed, the student must establish any other motives that are suggested in the documents. The phrasing of the question ('to what extent') also invites the student to consider whether the evidence contained in the documents is altogether reliable.]

Source C deals with the notable case in the last years of Henry's reign in which Lord Burgavenny was prosecuted for illegal retaining. At first sight the enormous fine involved may suggest that Henry was indeed motivated by financial greed. A closer reading shows, however, that the King is setting aside the bulk of this fine, and settling for a part payment of it, payable over a long period. The fact that, by accepting this recognisance, Lord Burgavenny admits his liability to imprisonment and confiscation of land illustrates that the document is intended more as a long-term threat than as an immediate punishment.

Similarly, in Source D, Edmund Dudley refers to a number of cases in which significant sums of money are concerned. Here too, however, it is not always clear that these sums were paid to the King. In the cases of Hawkins, Hubbard and others, the money does appear to have been handed over. Yet the Bishop of London was merely under 'obligation' and 'recognisance' to pay, while the Earl of Northumberland was treated in a manner similar to Lord Burgavenny. In the preamble to the document, Dudley asserts that Henry's primary purpose was in fact 'to have many persons in his danger at his pleasure'.

There is little reason not to take Source C, as a legal document, at face value. Source D may be seen as having an ulterior motive, for Dudley was under sentence of death at this time, and eager to cooperate with the new King. Nevertheless, our background knowledge informs us that such cases did exist. The conclusion that arises from these sources, therefore, is ambiguous. While they constitute a clear legal and political threat to several of his leading subjects, it is also clear that Henry VII did derive large sums of money from this practice, if not the enormous sums usually associated with the case of Lord Burgavenny.

SOURCES

2. THE QUESTION OF LEGITIMATE ROYAL AUTHORITY, 1546–53

Source G: part of the last will of Henry VIII, 30 December 1546.

And if it fortune our said daughter Mary to die without issue of her body lawfully begotten; we will that after our decease, and for default of the several bodies of us, and of our said son Prince Edward lawfully begotten, and of our daughter, Mary, the said imperial crown shall wholly remain and come to our said daughter Elizabeth, and to the heirs of her body lawfully begotten.

And if it shall fortune our said daughter Elizabeth to die without issue of her body lawfully begotten, the said imperial crown shall wholly remain and come to the heirs of the body of the Lady Frances our niece, eldest daughter to our late sister the French Queen; and for default of such issue, we will that the said imperial crown shall wholly remain and come to the heirs of the body of the Lady Eleanor our niece, second daughter of our said late sister the French Queen.

Source H: part of Edward VI's Letters Patent for the Limitation of the Crown, June 1553.

Forasmuch as the marriage had between our said late father and the Lady Catherine, mother to the said Lady Mary, was clearly and lawfully undone; and likewise the marriage had between our said late father and the Lady Anne, mother to the said Lady Elizabeth, was also clearly and lawfully undone. Whereby as well the said Lady Mary as also the said Lady Elizabeth to all intents and purposes are and be clearly disabled to ask, claim, or challenge the said imperial crown, and also for that the said Lady Mary and Lady Elizabeth be unto us but of the half blood, and therefore by the ancient laws, statutes and customs of this realm be not inheritable unto us, although they were legitimate, as they be not indeed.

Source I: part of an eye-witness account written by Baptista Spinola, a Genoese merchant in London, in July 1553.

Today I saw Lady Jane Grey walking in a grand procession to the Tower. She is now called Queen, but it is not popular, for the hearts of the people are with Mary, the Spanish Queen's daughter. She walked under a canopy, her mother carrying her long train, and her husband Guildford [Dudley] walking by her, dressed all in white and gold, a very tall strong boy, who paid her much attention. Many ladies followed, with noblemen, but this lady is very heretical and has never heard Mass, and some great people did not come into the procession for that reason.

Source J: part of a letter written by Elizabeth to the Duke of Northumberland, July 1553.

My sister and I were, some days ago, apprized of the plots which your ambition for the advancement of your own house has led you to form, in order to exclude us both from the succession to the crown. Now, why do you do us this injustice? Is it to call to the inheritance of the crown persons more remotely allied, of other blood, and other name, merely because they are your relations? Is this the fair renown that the King, our dear brother and sovereign lord, will, through your mad passion, leave behind? Is this the mighty honour your Lordship will gain – to make use of your present power, only to exclude from the succession the rightful daughters of King Henry our father, and the sisters on the father's side of King Edward, to bring in the daughter of the Duke of Suffolk, who has no claim than that of having married one of our aunts?

We hope that the Parliament and the judges, who are the defenders of the laws and of the crown, will drag us out of the oppression into which your ambition has cast us.

Source K: part of the letter written by the Privy Council to Mary in reply to her claim to the throne upon the death of Edward VI, 9 July 1553.

Madam, we have received your letter the ix of this instant declaring your supposed title which you judge yourself to have: the Imperial Crown of this Realm and all the domaines thereunto belonging. Our answer whereof is to advise you forasmuch as our Sovereign Lady Queen Jane is after the death of our Sovereign Lord King Edward VI, a prince of most noble memory, invested and possessed with right and just title in the Imperial Crown of this Realm, not only by good order of old ancient laws of this realm, but also by your late Sovereign Lord's letters patent signed with his own hand and sealed with the Great Seal of England in the presence of the most part of the nobles and councillors, judges and diverse other grown and sage persons assenting and subscribing unto the same.

Source L: part of An Act Declaring Queen Mary Legitimate, 1553.

Be it enacted by the authority of this present Parliament that all and every decree, sentence and judgement of divorce and separation between the King your father and the Queen your mother and all the process commenced, given or promulgated by Thomas Cranmer, then Archbishop of Canterbury, whereby the most just, pure and lawful marriage between the said late King your father and the said late Queen your mother was pronounced unlawful or unjust, be utterly nought, void and annihilate, as if the same had never been given or pronounced.

Questions

1. Explain the following references that occur in these documents: 'our late sister the French Queen' (Source G); 'the Lady Anne' (Source H); 'the Imperial Crown of this Realm' (Source K).
2. In what ways does Source H contradict Source G? How strong do you think the legal and constitutional grounds were for this contradiction?
*3. In the light of Sources I, J and K summarise the strengths and weaknesses of Jane Grey's position in July 1553.
4. 'Mary succeeded in her bid for the throne in 1553 because she was a Tudor. All other arguments had little effect upon the issue.' To what extent does the evidence in these sources support this statement?

Worked answer

*3 [The question requires both an examination of the sources and the application of some background knowledge. Such knowledge will enable the student to identify those elements in the sources that would have been influential in attaching men to, or detaching them from, the cause of Lady Jane Grey. It would be equally appropriate to answer the question 'source-by-source' or to summarise 'strengths' and 'weaknesses' in separate paragraphs.]

Only Source K suggests that the position of 'Queen Jane' in early July 1553 was tenable. In it the members of the Privy Council support her claim against that of Mary Tudor, suggesting that she had the backing of the leading political figures of the realm. One of the grounds that they cite also suggests that Jane's position was secure, for it rested upon the expressed will of the late King, Edward VI. Their other justifications, however, are less impressive, and the references to 'old ancient laws of this realm' are too general to be authoritative.

Against this, Sources I and J draw attention to forces that undermined Jane Grey's position. Spinola reports that 'the hearts of the people are with Mary', although it is not clear what authority he has for such a sweeping statement. He also indicates that Jane was too closely associated in people's minds with Protestantism to command the support of many influential Englishmen. Once again, although he produces little evidence in support of this claim, it is broadly supported by background knowledge of the period. Princess Elizabeth, in Source J, puts her finger on what was probably Jane Grey's major weakness. Her dynastic links to the Tudor dynasty were considerably weaker than those of either Elizabeth or Mary. While these could claim direct descent from Henry VIII, Jane's father, the Duke of Suffolk, had no better claim to royalty 'than that of having married one of our aunts'. Elizabeth's letter also expresses the popular view that Jane's candidature to the throne was part of a megalomaniac conspiracy on the part of the Duke of Northumberland, a perception that certainly did much to turn opinion against her.

2

COURT AND PATRONAGE

BACKGROUND NARRATIVE

For the greater part of the twentieth century historians approached the study of Tudor government through its formal institutions. In recent decades, however, they have appreciated more clearly that the political life of Tudor England was not determined solely, or even primarily, by parliamentary statutes or by permanent organs of government. Power also consisted of such informal elements as the favour of the monarch or of a chief minister, and the ability to maintain a following by providing favours in turn for one's own friends and clients. If Parliament or the law courts represented the formal means of government, the primary focus of this informal power was found in the royal Court. The Court of a Tudor monarch was unlike anything that medieval kings had known. The Tudors spent less time in the saddle, fighting wars or crushing rebellions in person, and the Court became less mobile, centred upon the many royal palaces that encircled London. It was to these palaces that the great men of the realm gravitated if they desired the rewards that derived from proximity to the ruler. 'One of the most striking political successes of the Tudors', David Loades has claimed, 'was the extent to which they succeeded in making their Court the centre of the aristocratic world.' (1)

Quite apart from the fact that the monarch conducted a large amount of formal government business there, meeting with the Council, the Court provided at least three important elements in the government of the realm. By far the most important of these political functions of the Court was its role in the distribution of patronage. This distribution of favours, and grants of lands or offices, could only be secured by access to the monarch, or to the great men of the realm, in whose gift they lay. 'Patronage', in Rosemary O'Day's words, 'made the early modern world turn round. He who possessed patronage possessed power – power to control people, politics and events; power to delegate power; power to command respect.' (2) A man like Lord Burghley, with a vast range of appointments and resources in his gift, would inevitably attract ambitious and able followers in all parts of the realm, and would thus be a formidable political figure. Those who enjoyed the favour of such great men could in turn enjoy prestige and dispense patronage in their localities, building up bases of power there that derived directly from, and were directly dependent upon the Court and the crown. Such community of interests among the governing classes was probably far more important than the passage of new statutes in ensuring the stability of English government for most of the sixteenth century.

The Court also served as a framework for the display of power and prowess that advertised the visible strength and authority of the monarch. The semi-public life of the Presence Chamber provided the monarch with a framework in which to establish and project an image, dazzling courtiers or more occasional visitors with splendid entertainments and displays. These served, in David Starkey's phrase, as 'the principal shop-window of monarchy'. In the Court of Henry VIII, elaborate jousts provided a manly substitute for the battlefield, and the career of Charles Brandon, who rose to the dignity of Duke of Suffolk, demonstrated the political rewards that might accrue to the King's favourite jousting partners. Henry's Court, like that of Elizabeth, also served as a cultural centre. Their music, masques, and indeed the architecture and decoration of the palaces themselves reflected the fashions of Renaissance Europe, and transmitted them on into the noble households of the provinces. It is important to remember in this respect that the Tudor Court was not entirely static. Henry VIII, and more particularly Elizabeth, spent many summers on 'progress'. Travelling about the Home Counties (rarely further afield), they combined display and patronage, showing themselves to their subjects, and honouring local dignitaries, many of whom lacked the time or the resources to wait upon the monarch in London. The principle remained the same: by dispensing such marks of favour, the monarch strengthened the local prestige, and thus the local influence, of those faithful to the government.

While the Presence Chamber was the focus of the monarch's display, the Privy Chamber in the reign of Henry VIII became a focus of real political influence and power. The courtiers who accompanied and served the King in these private apartments might hold no major office of state, but their intimate access to the monarch, and the obvious confidence that he displayed in them, made them political figures of the first importance. They were men whose favour it was worthwhile to cultivate. The importance of the Privy Chamber is illustrated by the growing political influence of the officers who served in it and controlled access to it. Above all, the Groom of the Stool, at first merely the servant who accompanied the King to the toilet, acquired enormous political influence by the end of Henry VIII's reign. This was most evident in 1546–47 when Sir Anthony Denny used the office, with its control over access to the King and to the royal signature, to facilitate Edward Seymour's political triumph. Later, in the reign of Edward VI, Sir John Gates emerged as a major political figure, based in the Privy Chamber, and able to control access to the young King on behalf of his patron, the Duke of Northumberland. The succession of two consecutive female monarchs, however, automatically implied the expulsion of male attendants from the Privy Chamber. The change abruptly reduced the significance of the institution, and forced major readjustments in the conduct of Tudor political life.

ANALYSIS (1): HOW DID THOMAS WOLSEY MAINTAIN HIS PRE-EMINENT POSITION IN ENGLISH POLITICS FOR SO LONG?

Historians traditionally divide Henry VIII's reign into two contrasting sections. While the second is full of upheaval, of radical legislation, the questioning of religious certainties, and the rise and fall of wives and ministers, the earlier period is characterised by stability and continuity. It was dominated by the career of Thomas Wolsey, raised rapidly by his monarch to the highest political office in the realm, and maintained there for a decade and half. Yet this great minister has not enjoyed a good 'press' from historians. Identified with Rome when his successors presided over the birth of an English Church, and with traditional methods of administration when Thomas Cromwell may have initiated a 'revolution in government', Wolsey has often been dismissed as an obstacle to enlightened policies. It has not been easy for historians to explain why he was maintained in office for so long by a traditionally capricious monarch. The modern reader of A.F. Pollard, (3) in particular, might wonder how, if Henry was indeed 'a man of cosmic genius', (4) and if Wolsey was primarily driven by his own political and ecclesiastical ambitions, so great a King could be deceived by so unworthy a servant. G.R. Elton (5) tackled this problem by making a much less favourable assessment of the King. Seeing Henry as a weaker and lazier man, happy to delegate the tiresome burdens of administration to a highly efficient minister, he resolved the problem without greatly enhancing Wolsey's reputation. At least Pollard and Elton gave the minister credit for his extraordinary industry and his remarkable powers of organisation and concentration. This was a man who might rise 'early in the morning about four of the clock, sitting down to write letters into England unto the King until four of the clock in the afternoon'. This picture, conveyed by George Cavendish (6), has never been challenged, but contemporaries and historians alike have sought a broader base than this for such an outstanding career.

By concentrating less upon policies, and more upon the Court and the personal relationships within it, a recent generation of historians has provided a more satisfactory explanation of Wolsey's success. These have paid much attention, for instance, to his working relationship with the other great men of the realm, with noblemen who considered themselves entitled to a share in political power. Polydore Vergil, (7) writing shortly after Wolsey's fall, established the enduring tradition that this relationship was based upon confrontation, that the Cardinal used his influence with the King to suppress the nobility and to keep them from challenging his position. In this account, Wolsey's greatest victory was over the Duke of Buckingham, dramatically convicted of treason and executed in 1521. Less dramatic, but equally effective, was the consistent employment of the Duke of Norfolk on military campaigns far from Court, on the Scottish borders or in Ireland. Hugely influential in the past, Vergil's interpretation has been recognised for some time as heavily biased against Wolsey, and recent historians have largely revised it. While Professor Elton saw the hand of a suspicious King behind the destruction of Buckingham, Peter Gwyn (8) and David Starkey (9) both accept that he was not only at odds with Wolsey, but with much of the political establishment. His fall resulted, therefore, largely from his own political miscalculations and indiscretion. Similarly, Norfolk's prolonged absences from Court may be seen as the natural form of employment for a senior nobleman with proven military talents. Peter Gwyn, indeed, has drawn attention to evidence that exists for a positive relationship between Wolsey and the nobility. The Grey and the Howard families, he points out, both sought his intervention in inheritance cases, and Charles Brandon famously sought his intervention after his controversial marriage to Henry's sister appeared to endanger his place in the King's favour. Many noble families also sent their offspring to be brought up and trained in the Cardinal's household. 'It is unlikely', claims Gwyn, 'that Wolsey ever felt seriously threatened by other members of the political elite.' Yet many writers would accept an alternative interpretation, that members of the nobility sought his favour out of necessity while he was so powerful, yet nevertheless resented his monopoly of power, and turned on him once he had lost the favour of the King.

Relatively little is known about the role of patronage in the maintenance of Wolsey's power. There is little evidence to suggest that Wolsey had any great degree of control over the distribution of royal patronage, or that Henry consistently followed his advice in such matters. Indeed, in a famous case in 1528, the Cardinal made a serious error in judgement by attempting to install his own candidate as Abbess of Wilton, when the King had clearly expressed his preference for another. It is clear, on the other hand, that Wolsey's own court, centred upon Hampton Court or upon York Place, provided a magnet for those who sought political preferment or similar favours. The famous jibes of John Skelton about Hampton Court outshining the King's Court were intended to undermine Wolsey. For our purposes, however, his claim that 'the King's court should have the excellence, but Hampton Court hath the pre-eminence' illustrates a contemporary perception that must have greatly enhanced the Cardinal's political importance.

David Starkey does not share Peter Gwyn's optimism about Wolsey's political security. In his work on the Privy Chamber he has outlined how, between 1515 and 1518, men such as Nicholas Carew, William Carey and Francis Bryan made the transition from being the King's boon companions and jousting partners to staffing his private apartments and becoming key political agents and advisers. Charismatic young men, so frequently in the King's company, and on such friendly terms with him, posed a political threat that Wolsey could not afford to ignore, and Starkey is convinced that the deflection of this threat constituted one of Wolsey's great political successes. He scored a number of great victories over the favourites of the Privy Chamber. In 1518–19 he focused Henry's enthusiasm upon a programme of administrative reforms, persuaded the King to pack off the 'minions' to Calais in honourable exile, and replaced them in the Privy Chamber with his own candidates. The recall of Henry's favourites later in 1519 was offset by a spell of frantic diplomatic and military activity, which involved their employment on distant embassies and campaigns. Wolsey's victory was then sealed by an extensive programme for reform of the royal household, known as the Ordinances of Eltham (1526). This involved the reduction of staff in many branches of the household, and the 'buying off' of certain members of the Privy Chamber with other lucrative posts and grants. Carew, Bryan and the influential Groom of the Stool, Sir William Compton, all left the Privy Chamber at this time.

Wolsey's ability to coexist with, or to overcome the opposition of, leading members of the Court and the political nation leads logically to the most important factor behind his long tenure of office; it depended entirely upon his relationship with the King. While that was largely obvious to contemporaries, recent authorities have begun to establish the complexity and the highly unusual nature of that relationship. There was certainly more to it than an industrious minister assuming the workload of a lazy king. 'Between 1515 and 1525,' John Guy (10) has concluded, 'it can be argued that Henry VIII treated him more as a partner than as a servant. For a decade Henry and Wolsey governed as a team.' The same writer provides a definition of Wolsey's policies that might serve equally well as a list of Henry's priorities: 'He was flexible and opportunist; he thought in European terms and on the grand scale. His policies had the effect of centralising English politics [so that] the firm rule of Henry VII was continued by different means, and political attention was focused on Westminster and the King's court.' Peter Gwyn only slightly modified Guy's main conclusion when he compared the relationship to that in a modern company between the chairman and the managing director. Professor Scarisbrick, (11) however, defined the relationship in more complex terms. Wolsey, in his view, was always the more dominant figure in personal terms, while Henry never surrendered or forgot his political primacy. 'Wolsey's was the keener mind,' he argued, 'and certainly the firmer will – with the result that for a dozen years Henry's dependence upon him, though erratic, was often childlike.' Yet Henry, even if he was often bored by detail, was rarely a passive figure in political decision making, and he always remained 'the true source of the really important events of the reign'.

Such a relationship forced Wolsey to maintain a most delicate balance in order to maintain his position. In Scarisbrick's definition he had to be 'servant yet master, creature yet impresario; he must abase himself and yet dominate, playing a part which only a man of superlative energy, self-confidence and loyalty could have endured.'

The nature of Wolsey's fall helps to confirm this interpretation. He did not fall because he was ousted by another minister, or by gentlemen of the Privy Chamber, or by a jealous nobility. Instead, he fell because the King found someone more valuable to him than his Cardinal, and Wolsey could not counteract the kind of influence that Anne Boleyn exerted over Henry. The combination of Henry's passion and Wolsey's failure to annul the existing marriage to Queen Catherine destroyed the relationship upon which his power depended. Deprived of the King's trust and affection, he was destroyed by a formidable coalition of rivals, Boleyn supporters, disgruntled former 'minions' and conservative aristocratic councillors who had nothing more in common than their shared desire to gain a share of his political authority.

The long career of Thomas Wolsey teaches many lessons about the nature of early Tudor government. The debate that once preoccupied historians, whether policy originated with the King or with his chief minister, obscured the fact that the will of the King was the only thing that mattered. It could, of course, be influenced, changed and directed, and the politics of the Court and of the palace were largely concerned with those processes. It was a game that Thomas Wolsey played with consummate skill, and therein lies the secret of his two decades of political dominance. Wolsey was, indeed, in Skelton's phrase, 'the King's darling', trusted and supported by Henry, and generally giving substance and detail to broad lines of policy that he knew to be acceptable to the King.

Questions

1. How fair is the judgement that 'Thomas Wolsey's greatest talent was as a political survivor'?
2. Why did Wolsey's political authority last so long, and then end so suddenly in 1529?

ANALYSIS (2): WHAT WAS THE IMPACT OF ELIZABETH'S REIGN UPON COURT POLITICS AND PATRONAGE?

Elizabeth was not, of course, the first woman to sit upon the English throne, but her reign cannot easily be compared to that of her predecessor. Mary's reign was brief, the Queen had little taste for public display, and her decision to marry Philip of Spain raised the possibility that her Court might, after all, have a traditional, male focus. The length of Elizabeth's reign, together with her celibacy, raised a host of issues that her half-sister did not have to confront.

The most obvious implication of a female succession was that the Privy Chamber could not maintain the fundamental political importance that it had acquired under Henry VIII. Men were now excluded from the positions closest to the Queen's person and she was surrounded by female servants unable to exercise the overtly political roles played by their menfolk. Besides, Elizabeth's Privy Chamber remained 'virtually a closed shop' throughout the reign, with membership largely limited to a small group of families, such as the Howards, the Careys, and the Knollys, with whom the Queen had links of blood or of long-term loyalty. Under Henry VIII, Pam Wright (12) has concluded, 'the Privy Chamber had been the cockpit of faction. Elizabeth knew none of this. As women, her Ladies could not be faction leaders: their first loyalties were to the Queen, not to one of her great men.'

It is not quite clear, however, whether this Privy Chamber was entirely apolitical. At times important contemporaries grumbled about the political interference of the Queen's ladies. Leicester believed in 1569 that Norfolk's plans to marry Mary Stuart had been revealed to the Queen, and thus frustrated, by 'some babbling women' in the Privy Chamber, and Sir Walter Raleigh complained similarly that the ladies were 'capable of doing great harm but no good' in political matters. There is much wider evidence that the ladies frequently used their proximity to the Queen to seek favours on behalf of a relative or friend. Recent writers have usually resolved this problem by separating patronage from politics. While the granting of favours did nothing to erode her personal authority, Elizabeth seems energetically to have resisted any penetration of male, high politics into the Privy Chamber. It may be that the Queen's concern to keep politics out of the Privy Chamber helps to explain her well-known hostility towards the marriage projects of her ladies. This is often interpreted as part of the Queen's reaction to her own sexual frustration, but perhaps, as Pam Wright suggests, it arose in part from Elizabeth's determination that courtly faction should not penetrate her household through the husbands of the women who surrounded her. Christopher Haigh (13) takes a compromise position, noting the importance that Elizabeth attached to her status as the 'sexual focus' of the Court, and resenting any competition in this respect from her ladies. 'It did the reputation of the Virgin Queen no good if the Maids kept getting pregnant.'

The exclusion of national politics from the Queen's private apartments perhaps had two important implications for the politics of the Court and the government of the realm at large. Pam Wright has argued that, because the access of male administrators to the Queen was now so strictly limited, many of the administrative tasks that the Privy Chamber had taken on under Henry VIII reverted to officers outside the household. The chief beneficiary was William Cecil, Lord Burghley, (14) whose extensive and durable political authority, unchallenged by alternative political influences within the Queen's apartments, was one of the distinctive features of the reign. With the lapsing of such household financial offices as Keeper of the Privy Purse and Keeper of the Royal Coffers, Burghley also gained much greater control of the purse strings. 'The same', Pam Wright argues, 'went for the obtaining of the Queen's signature – the prime motor of government. Here the informal free-for-almost-anyone-who-mattered of Henry VIII's reign was replaced by increased formalisation and bureaucracy.' In his capacity as Principal Secretary, Burghley was again the major beneficiary.

On the other hand, Burghley and his ministerial colleagues had to contend with the influence, as a direct result of the monarch's gender, of a new kind of political rival. There arose a new kind of Court favourite, 'the male favourite', in Simon Adams's words, (15) whose leading characteristic was his physical and personal attraction for the Queen. The most notable examples, of course, were Robert Dudley, Earl of Leicester, and Robert Devereux, Earl of Essex, although Sir Christopher Hatton and Sir Walter Raleigh might be added to that list. Some historians have been convinced that the emergence of such favourites made Elizabeth's Court the scene of factional struggles every bit as profound as those of earlier reigns. Sir John Neale (16) pictured Burghley and Leicester locked for much of the reign in a fierce personal rivalry over the direction of royal patronage. While Burghley could base his power upon his control of administration, he could never effectively counteract the personal bond that existed between Elizabeth and Leicester. More recent writers have tended to play down such rivalry. Wallace MacCaffrey (17) accepted the existence of rivalry over the distribution of patronage, but felt that it was largely confined to the earlier years of the reign, when Leicester could still entertain hopes of a marriage to Elizabeth. Once such hopes had faded, however, Burghley's position was secure and the interests of the two great men were better able to coexist. Christopher Haigh largely supports this argument by demonstrating that Burghley and Leicester exercised their patronage in different areas of the body politic. Vast as his patronage was, particularly in the matter of parliamentary elections, Burghley enjoyed little influence over church or university appointments, areas in which Leicester was dominant. Simon Adams builds further upon this theme, arguing that the limited rivalry of Burghley and Leicester was of little significance when set against the circumstances of the older, largely Catholic aristocracy, who were excluded from the profits of Court and patronage by the Protestant elite that now held power. The Duke of Norfolk provides the classic case of a great provincial magnate, in decline because he was denied royal patronage. His alternative plans to enhance his political influence by marriage to the heir apparent led (1569–72) to his downfall and execution.

In addition to these political aspects of the Court, it was inevitable that its display functions would also change now that a Queen sat on the throne. While cultural historians have written a great deal about the artistic merits of the tilts, masques and other entertainments that were a regular feature of Court life, we must concentrate more upon their political significance. Elizabeth's ministers were faced with the novel and difficult task of creating a credible, majestic image for a female monarch, and the culture of the Court was one of the most important vehicles for doing so. Christopher Haigh has summarised the philosophy that was eventually applied to solve this problem. 'Elizabeth was both *above* the Court, as a sovereign claiming the fealty of her knights, and *of* the Court, as the virgin lady for whose honour knights fought at the tilt. The Court served as a splendid palace for the display of majesty, but also as a more intimate forum for romantic play-acting and political seduction.' Building upon the medieval conventions of 'courtly love' (18) she accepted and developed the role of the female monarch as the desirable, yet unattainable, sexual focus of the Court. It took some time to develop what Penry Williams (19) has described as 'ceremonies of adoration', but he attaches much importance to the Accession Day Tilts of 1578 as marking the emergence of the image of the 'Virgin Queen'. Others have seen it as a somewhat slower process. Simon Adams believes that it was not until after 1580 that Court culture 'entered a particularly intense phase, coinciding with the spread of the Gloriana cult (and her own acceptance of the role) and the growing formality of ceremonial'. (20) Whatever the pace of the process, there is ample evidence in the reports of foreign ambassadors and other occasional visitors to Court to suggest that such display had the desired effect.

Are we to conclude from this that the adaptation of Elizabeth's Court was a complete success, enhancing the stability and the government of the realm? In answering this question it is probably important not to treat Elizabeth's long reign as a whole. John Guy (21) has offered us the concept of 'Elizabeth's second reign', occupying the years between 1585 and 1603, which saw the disappearance of many successful and influential courtiers, including Leicester (d.1588) and Hatton (d.1591). Most important of all, the decline and death of Burghley (d.1598) seemed to open the real possibility of a more even contest for influence and patronage at Court. The Queen, too, grew more conservative, becoming, as Sir John Harington described her, 'a lady shut up in a chamber from her subjects and most of her servants, and seldom seen but on holy days'. Having encouraged flirtation and ritualised sexuality as a route to political favour, the elderly Elizabeth seems to have changed the rules of the courtly 'game'. Although she continued to use flirtation as a factional weapon, she had detached political power from it: 'she flirted with Essex and Raleigh,' writes Haigh, 'but made decisions with Buckhurst and Cecil. Her affection was now politically worthless.' The tensions thus generated eventually erupted in intrigue and violence. The young Earl of Essex, the new 'male favourite', and the men who followed him because he appeared to enjoy the Queen's favour, experienced a degree of political and financial frustration that culminated in his disastrous rebellion in 1601. In this respect, as in others, the last years of the reign represented decline and stagnation. In Haigh's graphic phrase, 'the Court which had been the scene of Gloriana's splendour became a sordid and self-seeking playpen for overgrown and ill-tempered children'.

Questions

1. 'In the course of her reign Elizabeth firmly established the credibility of female monarchy.' How accurate is this judgement?
2. How strong is the case for arguing that, under Elizabeth, the Court was governed more effectively than the country at large?

SOURCES

1. THE RELATIONSHIP BETWEEN THOMAS WOLSEY AND HENRY VIII

Source A: from the biography of Thomas Wolsey, written by his gentleman-usher, George Cavendish. In this extract Cavendish describes the reasons for Wolsey's initial rise in the King's favour.

And whereas the other ancient councillors would, according to the office of good councillors, diverse times persuade the King to have sometime an intercourse into the council, there to hear what was done in weighty matters, the which pleased the King nothing at all, for he loved nothing worse than to be constrained to do anything contrary to his royal will and pleasure; and that knew the almoner very well, having a secret intelligence [knowledge] of the King's natural inclination, and so fast as the other councillors advised the King to leave his pleasure, and to attend to the affairs of the realm, so busily did the almoner persuade him to the contrary; which delighted him much, and caused him to have the greater affection and love to the almoner. Who was now in high favour, but Master Almoner? Who had all the suit, but Master Almoner? And who ruled all under the King, but Master Almoner?

Source B: an extract from *Anglica Historia*, an account of the reign by the Italian humanist Polydore Vergil. He was a persistent enemy of Wolsey and spent some time in prison as a result.

Every time that he wished to obtain something from Henry, he [Wolsey] introduced the matter casually into his conversation; then he brought out some small present or another, a beautifully fashioned dish, for example, or a jewel or ring or gifts of that sort, and while the King was admiring the gift intently, Wolsey would adroitly bring forward the project on which his mind was fixed.

Source C: from one of the many satires that John Skelton wrote against Wolsey. Skelton, a client and protégé of the Duke of Norfolk, wonders at the extent of Wolsey's influence over the King.

It is a wondrous case:
That the King's grace
Is towards him so minded,
And so far blinded,
That he cannot perceive,
How he doth him deceive,

I doubt lest by sorcery,
Or such other loselry, [something of no worth]
As witchcraft or charming;
For he is the King's darling.

Source D: from a letter written by the Venetian ambassador to the Venetian Senate, 1519.

Within the last few days, His Majesty has made a very great change in the Court here, dismissing four of his chief lords-in-waiting, who enjoyed extreme authority in the kingdom, and were the very soul of the King. He has likewise changed some other officials, replacing them by men of greater age and repute, a matter which is deemed of as vital importance as any that has taken place for many years. The French ambassador considers that this took place either from suspicion about the affairs of France, or at the instigation of Cardinal Wolsey, who, perceiving the aforesaid to be so intimate with the King that in the course of time they might have ousted him from the government, anticipated them, under pretence of their being youths of evil counsel, an opinion which I fully share. By this, the said Cardinal of York will secure the King entirely to himself, extremely to the displeasure of all the grandees of the kingdom.

Source E: part of a letter written by Henry VIII to Wolsey, probably in 1520.

Mine own good Cardinal, I recommend me unto you as heartily as heart can think. So it is because writing to me is somewhat tedious and painful, therefore the most part of this business I have committed to our trusty councillor, this bearer, to be declared to you by mouth, to which we would you should give credence. Nevertheless, to this that followeth I thought not best to make him privy, nor none other but you and I, which is that I would you should make good watch on the Duke of Suffolk, on the Duke of Buckingham, on my lord of Northumberland, on my lord of Derby, on my lord of Wiltshire and on others which you think suspect, to see what they do with this news. No more to you at this time. Writing with the hand of your loving master. Henry R.

Source F: Cavendish's report of a conversation between Wolsey and Sir William Kingston, at the time of Wolsey's arrest in 1529.

The king is a prince of royal courage, and hath a princely heart; and rather that he will either miss or want any part of his will or appetite, he will put the loss of one half of his realm in danger. For I assure you that I have often kneeled before him in his privy chamber on my knees the space of an hour or two to persuade him from his will and appetite; but I could never bring to pass to dissuade him therefrom. Therefore, Master Kingston, if it chance hereafter you to be one of his privy council, I warn you to be well advised and assured what matter ye put into his head; for ye shall never pull it out again.

Questions

1. Explain the following terms that occur in these sources: 'the other councillors' (Source A); 'Master Almoner' (Source A); 'suspicion about the affairs of France' (Source D).
*2. Sources A, B and C all provide different explanations for Wolsey's influence with Henry. What is the relative value to the present-day historian of each of these explanations?
3. What impression do you gain from Sources E and F about Henry VIII's style of government?
4. The Venetian ambassador described Wolsey as 'alter rex' ('the other king'). To what extent do these documents, and any other evidence known to you, support the assertion that Wolsey was Henry's equal in terms of political authority?

Worked answer

*2. [Although it might be worthwhile for the student to make clear that he/she recognises the explanation that each source gives for Wolsey's influence over the King, the main emphasis is upon evaluation of the sources. An adequate answer must at least comment upon the relative authority of each author, and must try to identify any bias that might have distorted their views. To answer the question well, the student should go on to consider what the modern historian may learn from each source, even if it is subjective in its views.]

The sources provide a variety of explanations for the influence that Cardinal Wolsey was able to exercise over Henry VIII. Cavendish attributes it largely to Wolsey's shrewd assessment of the King's character, and especially to Henry's aversion to hard work, while Polydore Vergil ascribes it to the cunning that the minister showed in introducing his policies and projects to the royal attention. Skelton, apparently amazed that the King can be so deceived by an unworthy servant, can only assume that Wolsey has used magic to bewitch the King.

None of the explanations can be taken absolutely at face value. Cavendish, as a close household servant of Wolsey, may be in the best position to know the truth. He may have heard this explanation directly from the Cardinal, although that does not make it absolutely reliable.

On the other hand, his biography of his former master was under-standably sympathetic, and could lead us to suspect that Wolsey is often shown in a flattering light. The reverse is very largely true of Polydore Vergil's testimony in Source B. The Italian is well known to have been hostile to Wolsey, and he is habitually critical of him in his *Anglica Historia*. It is by no means clear where he would have got the information that he conveys in this source. On the other hand, it would be unwise to assume that everything written by a politician's enemies is untrue, and it is perfectly plausible to assume that an ambitious royal servant might have acted in this way. Skelton, finally, is certainly not telling the truth, and it is not acceptable to the modern historian to be told that Wolsey controlled Henry VIII by witchcraft. Yet the source is not without value to the historian. Quite apart from the fact that such a charge would have been much more credible in the early sixteenth century, the source also illustrates the frustration of the Cardinal's political enemies, and the extent to which they might go to explain Wolsey's influence without giving him credit and without implying any criticism of the King.

SOURCES

2. ELIZABETH'S STYLE IN COURT AND GOVERNMENT

Source G: from Sir Robert Naunton's *Fragmenta Regalia*, published in 1641.

Bowyer, the gentleman of the Black Rod, being charged by her [Elizabeth's] express command to look precisely to all admissions in the Privy Chamber, one day stayed a very gay captain (and a follower of my Lord of Leicester) from entrance. Leicester coming to the contestation said publicly that he [Bowyer] was a knave and should not long continue in his office. Bowyer, who was a bold gentleman and well-beloved, stepped before him and fell at her Majesty's feet, relates the story and humbly craves her Grace's pleasure, and in such manner as if he demanded whether my Lord of Leicester was king or her Majesty Queen. Whereunto she replied (with her wonted oath – 'God's death'), 'My Lord, I have wished you well, but my favour is not so locked up for you that others shall not participate thereof. I will have here but one mistress, and no master, and look that no ill happen to him, lest it be severely required at your hands.' Which so quailed my Lord of Leicester that his feigned humility was, long after, one of his best virtues.

Source H: part of a letter from Sir Thomas Smith to Lord Burghley, March 1575.

For matters of state I will write as soon as I can have any access to her Majesty, the which, as it was when your Lordship was here sometime so, sometime no, and all times uncertain and ready to stays and revocation. This irresolution doth weary and kill her ministers, destroy her actions and overcome all good designs and counsels. No letters touching Ireland, although read and allowed by her Majesty, yet can I get signed. I wait whilst [until] I neither have eyes to see or legs to stand upon. For private matters and suits I have the same success. They increase daily. Yea nor nay can I get. We need within a while to have a horse or ass to carry the bills after us, increasing daily and never dispatched.

Source I: from an account of the English court written by Paul Hentzer, a Silesian who visited England in 1598. His journal, containing this account, was first published in 1617.

We were admitted to the Presence Chamber, hung with rich tapestry; at the door stood a gentleman in velvet, with a gold chain, whose office was to introduce to the Queen any person of distinction that came to wait on her. In the same hall were a great number of councillors of state and gentlemen who awaited the Queen's coming out, which she did from her own apartments when it was time to go to prayers. First came barons, earls, knights of the Garter, all richly dressed and bare-headed; next came the Chancellor, bearing the Seals in a red silk purse, between two others, one carrying the royal sceptre, the other the sword of state in a red scabbard with the point upwards. Next came the Queen, in the 65th year of her age, very majestic, her face fair but wrinkled, her eyes small yet black and pleasant, her nose a little hooked, her teeth black (from the English habit of too great use of sugar). Her air was stately, her manner of speaking mild and obliging. As she went along she spoke to one and another in English, French and Italian. The ladies of the court followed, very handsome and well-shaped. She was guarded on each side by fifty gentlemen with gilt battleaxes.

Source J: part of a letter from Sir Christopher Hatton to Elizabeth, written while he was away from Court on a diplomatic mission, 5 June 1573.

Madam, I find the greatest lack that ever poor wretch sustained. No death, no, not hell, no fear of death shall ever win of me my consent so far to wrong myself again as to be absent from you one day. God grant my return. I will perform this vow. I lack that [which] I live by. The further I go from you, the more I find this lack. My spirit and soul agreeth with my body and life, that to serve you is a heaven, but to lack you is more than hell's torment unto them. Would God I were with you but for one hour. My wits are overwrought with thoughts. I find myself amazed. Bear with me, my most dear sweet Lady. Passion overcometh me. I can write no more.

Source K: part of a memoir written by Geoffrey Goodman, a law student, December 1588.

I did then live in the Strand, near St Clement's Church, when suddenly there was a report that the Queen was gone to Council [at Somerset House], and I was told 'If you will see the Queen, you must come quickly.' Then we all ran, and there we stayed an hour and a half, and the yard was full, when the Queen came out in great state. Then we cried 'God save your Majesty.' And the Queen turned to us and said 'God bless you all, my good people.' And the Queen said again to us 'Ye may well have a greater prince, but ye shall never have a more loving prince.' And so the Queen and the crowd there, looking upon one another awhile, her Majesty departed. This wrought such an impression upon us that all the way long we did nothing but talk what an admirable Queen she was and how we would adventure our lives in her service.

Questions

1. Explain the following terms that occur in these sources: 'access to her Majesty' (Source H); 'the Presence Chamber' (Source I); 'bearing the Seals' (Source I).
*2. Sir Thomas Smith (Source H) and Sir Christopher Hatton (Source J) display very different attitudes towards Elizabeth. How would you account for this difference?
3. What evidence may be gained from Sources G, I and J about the means that Elizabeth employed to ensure her position as the focus of the Court?
4. 'Elizabeth was far more successful in her domination of her Court than in the political practicalities of government.' To what extent is this statement supported by these sources, and by other evidence known to you?

Worked answer

*2. [The question involves two tasks, one rather more difficult than the other. The student may usefully identify the different tones and moods in the two sources, but he/she will only gain a modest mark unless he/she can explain these differences. This may be done by considering the different purposes for which the two letters were written, and probably requires some background knowledge of the different relationships that might exist at Court between the Queen and her various ministers and courtiers.]

Sources H and J are both written by servants of the crown, engaged on state business, but their respective tones and moods contrast starkly with one other. Sir Thomas Smith is preoccupied with the bureaucratic routine of government, and writes in a mood of frustration. He describes to Burghley an indecisive Queen, who refuses to attend to business, and whose behaviour delays and disrupts the conduct of government. Sir Christopher Hatton, on the other hand, writes what is in effect a love letter, addressing the Queen as his 'dear sweet Lady', from whom he cannot bear to be parted. Above all, his claim that 'to serve you is a heaven' is in direct contrast with the impression that Smith gives of life in the Queen's service.

To understand this difference it is important to be aware that Sir Christopher Hatton was one of the 'male favourites' who rose to political prominence because of his attractiveness to Elizabeth, and because of his talents as a courtier. In his letter, he is observing the conventions of 'courtly love' which required the courtier to treat Elizabeth as the emotional and sexual focus of the Court. Sir Thomas Smith, on the other hand, is clearly a more pragmatic official whose work revolves around practical detail rather than ritualised courtship. His priority is the conduct of government policy rather than his own position in the Queen's affections. Moreover, his letter is written to Lord Burghley whose close relationship owed more to efficient administration than to physical attractions. The letter is not designed for Elizabeth's eyes and can therefore provide a more realistic account of the Queen's character and conduct, away from the 'image-creation' and 'image-projection' that played such important roles in Court life.

3

THE CENTRAL ORGANS AND OFFICES OF GOVERNMENT

BACKGROUND NARRATIVE

In a sense it is misleading to speak of organs of central government, especially in the early decades of Tudor administration. The personalities of leading ministers remained as important as the personality and priorities of the monarch and, in the formulation and execution of state policies, governmental organs and offices were usually no more effective than the individuals who occupied or constituted them.

Throughout the sixteenth century, the royal Council was the primary element in the government of the realm, essentially a collection of individual ministers in whom the monarch trusted or, in some cases, who possessed such expertise and/or influence that government could not effectively be carried on without them. Naturally this body has been of outstanding interest to constitutional historians of the period who have constructed the following orthodox model of its development. Henry VII's Council, once thought to have numbered as many as forty or fifty members, is now seen as an informal and shifting body, with a few select councillors attending regularly, while others were summoned to meetings when it suited the King's interests. Under Henry VIII the Council continued to consist of a select group of ministers, dominated at first by Thomas Wolsey but developing, in the 1530s, into a more formal body. This formalisation of the Council into an elite Privy Council of trusted, permanent members was interrupted during the less stable reigns of Edward VI and Mary. In this mid-Tudor period the Council once again witnessed factional struggles and, in Mary's reign in particular, suffered a decline in its direct influence over government policy, as the Queen turned to advisers outside the normal circle of state councillors. Elizabeth, however, reverted to a small and select Privy Council in which no member held office because of any semi-independent power base, but only because of the trust and esteem that he enjoyed in the eyes of the Queen.

Although the structure of the Council varied in the course of the sixteenth century, its role did not. Its major task was to provide the monarch with guidance upon any matter that he or she put before it. 'The outstanding characteristic of the Council was', as G.R. Elton wrote, 'its all-pervasiveness: nothing that happened within the realm appeared to fall outside its competence.' (1) Otherwise, the Council's business fell into two broad categories, administrative and judicial. Its administrative work might involve anything that arose within the realm, from military defence to the relief of the poor. Its judicial work changed as the century progressed, from the direct involvement of councillors such as Wolsey sitting in Star Chamber, to the reallocation of petitions and cases to more appropriate courts. Indeed, in 1582 it was formally decided that the Council would deal directly with no further legal cases unless they concerned the safety of the Queen and the realm.

Although the role of the Council changed little under the Tudors, important changes occurred in the roles of the great officers of state. The greatest minister in the early part of the sixteenth century was the Lord Chancellor, an office stabilised and magnified by the long tenures of John Morton (1487–1500), William Warham (1504–15) and Thomas Wolsey (1515–29). During this period the Chancellor was the monarch's chief minister and adviser, controlling the Great Seal by which the major decisions of government were validated, and dominating the administration of civil law. The public career of Thomas Cromwell, beginning in the 1530s, witnessed a shift of political emphasis to his own office of Secretary. Although this office was less clearly defined than that of Chancellor, and although it lost much of its influence when held by lesser men, in the hands of Cromwell (1533–40) and William Cecil (1550–53; 1558–72) the office was one from which English government could be dominated. This they achieved, not through their titles or through feudal precedence, but through the personal confidence that the monarch placed in them and the overview that they enjoyed over all aspects of government. The most successful of the Tudor Secretaries were skilful political managers, manipulating Court, Council and Parliament in the royal interest.

ANALYSIS (1): WHAT WAS THE IMPORTANCE AND EXTENT OF THOMAS CROMWELL'S WORK ON THE RESTRUCTURING OF TUDOR GOVERNMENT?

The study of the government of Tudor England has been dominated throughout the second half of the twentieth century by the debate generated by Geoffrey Elton's thesis of the 'Tudor revolution in government'. (2) Professor Elton's 'revolution' extended beyond the organs of central government to embrace the role of Parliament, the scope and authority of statute law, the royal Supremacy over the Church, and the extension of royal authority into the localities. Many of these issues feature in other sections of this book. Inevitably, he claimed, such an extension of royal authority necessitated a radical reorganisation of central government. In particular, Cromwell's administrative reforms embraced the royal Council, the office of the King's principal Secretary, and the financial institutions of the realm. In his relatively short period of influence, Thomas Cromwell transformed the government of the realm from a personal process, largely dependent upon the energy of the King and his leading ministers, into one carried out by the impersonal operations of a centralised bureaucracy. These changes, furthermore, were part of a deliberate and premeditated master plan.

Central to Elton's interpretation was the restructuring of the Council. In his view an informal body, variable in number and with its membership dependent upon the royal whim, was transformed in the 1530s. It became a formalised Privy Council, a select body of trusted ministers and office holders, about nineteen in number, which constituted by 1540 a distinct and permanent institution of government. At the same time the judicial functions of the Council were transferred to the Court of Star Chamber and to the Court of Requests, which now functioned as distinct institutions. There is general agreement that such changes did take place, but many writers refuse to see it as so rapid a process as Elton outlines, and reject his claims that Cromwell brought it about 'as a conscious act of administrative reform designed to modernise the existing King's Council'. John Guy (3) has argued instead that the transition had its origins in the crisis of 1536, generated by the fall of Anne Boleyn and the Pilgrimage of Grace. At this point the King's most trusted ministers met as an 'inner council', to the exclusion of others, as a pragmatic measure at a time of intense political danger, and not as a premeditated act of statesmanship. He notes that this select Council contained so many of Cromwell's political enemies, men who brought him down in 1540, that it cannot reasonably be seen as his ideal solution to governmental problems. In addition, the Council exercised its collective authority less as the crisis receded and Cromwell's confidence returned, and the practice was only resumed when the great minister fell from power. The permanent Privy Council took shape, Guy concludes, 'less because [Cromwell] lived than because he died'. David Starkey (4) adds to this the objection that, even then, the formalised Council of 1540 changed its form and its role in response to the political crises of the 1540s and 1550s, before settling back into its elite format in the reign of Elizabeth. Several writers also note the precedents for such reforms that existed in Wolsey's administration. Not only did the Cardinal greatly enhance the judicial role of Star Chamber, he proposed, but apparently never implemented, a similar reconstruction of the Council in the Ordinances of Eltham in 1526.

Alongside changes in the nature of the Council, Elton claimed, Cromwell transformed the office of Secretary. By virtue of his role in handling royal correspondence, and controlling the use of the King's private seal, the Secretary had considerable potential power, but in Cromwell's hands a relatively modest Household office was transformed into a great office of state. On this issue, subsequent writers have been more mild in their revision of Elton's interpretation. David Loades (5) accepts, for instance, that Cromwell's exploitation of the office was novel and that he 'deserves great credit for spotting the potentialities of regular and unchallenged access to the King's person'. Although Elton's critics do not deny that the office acquired much greater importance in Cromwell's hands, nor that William Cecil dominated government from the same position in the opening years of Elizabeth's reign, they point out that its significance declined in the intervening years. Upon Cromwell's fall, his office was divided between two lesser figures, Wriothesley and Sadler, and none of the seven men who occupied the office between 1540 and 1558 exercised such influence upon government as Cromwell had done. The conclusion is that the importance of Cromwell and of Cecil depended less upon the office that they held than upon the ability of each individual and the confidence placed in him by his monarch. Indeed, Elton later modified his original claims in this respect, arguing that 'Cromwell's secret lay in the infusion of personal authority into an office of very secondary importance. Although by no means all post-Cromwellian secretaries carried Cromwell's authority . . . the effect of his imprint endured.'

Cromwell engineered a substantial increase in royal income and catered for it by an important reorganisation of financial administration. He established the Court of Augmentations (1536) to handle income from the former monastic lands and the Court of Wards (1540) to deal with increased feudal revenues. The policy was extended after Cromwell's death by foundation of the Court of First Fruits and Tenths (1540) and the Court of General Surveyors (1542). This much is not open to doubt. Once again, however, later writers have questioned both the motivation and the effectiveness of Cromwell's work. For John Guy and Christopher Coleman, (6) Cromwell's aim was not so much efficient administration, but effective, personal control of state finance. Once he had fallen from power, it became increasingly clear that, far from enhancing the effectiveness of financial administration, Cromwell had created, in David Starkey's words, 'a complex, even chaotic financial machine'. In 1553–54 it was felt necessary to restore the authority of the Exchequer in order to restore the stability and efficiency of the financial system. Whether this was, as some contemporaries interpreted it, a return to 'the ancient course', or, as J.D. Alsop (7) has claimed, part of the consistent updating and modification of the Exchequer, the dominant financial institution of sixteenth-century monarchy, the significance of Cromwell's departmentalisation is diminished. Dr Alsop also draws attention to the personnel within these financial departments. He points out that the ease with which officials moved from one department to another, or worked in several at the same time, may indicate that Professor Elton exaggerated their separate, independent nature. John Guy adds to this the conclusion that, whatever the significance of Cromwell's administrative reforms, their overall aim was ultimately conservative; to re-endow the crown in order to provide it with the means to play its traditional roles of active foreign policy and effective dispensation of patronage.

Alongside the debates about specific elements in the 'revolution', David Starkey has criticised the central assumption that Cromwell sought deliberately to take government out of the hands of the royal Household. In his view, Cromwell was far less concerned with models of government, with the efficiency of Household administration, than with its implications for his own tenure of power. When he had control of Household procedures, as he had between the fall of Anne Boleyn (1536) and the beginning of his own fall (1539–40), he was content to allow them a leading role in government. Starkey also emphasises the continued influence exercised by officers of the Household in the final years of Henry's reign, as the King's health declined dramatically.

Overall, it remains undeniable that the middle years of the sixteenth century witnessed remarkable changes in royal authority and in the administration of the realm. In particular the powers of the crown were extended in the 1530s to a degree that could reasonably be described as 'revolutionary'. Yet, while Thomas Cromwell played a major role in bringing these changes about, it now seems excessive to ascribe revolutionary importance to his administrative reforms. The carefully balanced conclusion drawn by John Guy probably represents the current state of this debate: 'The thesis that a Tudor "revolution in government" took place is comprehensible when the periodisation of change is extended to Elizabeth's death, though whether the word "revolution" is appropriate – as opposed to "readjustment" or straightforward "change" – is a matter of judgement.'

Questions

1. To what extent is the concept of a 'Tudor revolution in government' still useful for the historian of Tudor England?
2. 'Overall, Cromwell's contribution to the government of Tudor England was more constructive than Wolsey's.' Do you agree?

ANALYSIS (2): HOW WELL WAS MARY TUDOR SERVED BY HER COUNCILLORS?

Historians of the sixteenth century have traditionally interpreted the reign of Mary Tudor as an aberration. Her return to Catholicism contrasted with the earlier impetus towards an independent English Church, and a pro-Habsburg foreign policy, while not unusual in itself, took on a new and sinister aspect once the English crown became bound by marriage to that of Spain. At the beginning of the twentieth century A.F. Pollard (8) added the judgement that the sterility and confusion of Mary's reign were compounded by a virtual collapse in the structure of conciliar government. In Pollard's view a Queen who needed guidance more than most was inadequately advised by a Council that was too large, bitterly divided along factional lines, and fundamentally mediocre in its political talents.

It is certainly true that Mary faced unprecedented difficulties over the formation of her Council. Of the men who had guided Henry VIII and Edward VI over the past decade some were automatically disqualified by their involvement in Northumberland's treasonable attempt to exclude Mary from the succession. Others, such as Paget, Petre, Winchester, Arundel and Pembroke, were not so severely compromised, but they had been closely involved in the recent assault upon the Catholic religion that was so close to the Queen's heart. Stephen Gardiner represented a third category, clearly hostile to the Protestant trends of Edward's reign, yet formerly faithful servant of Henry VIII in his attack upon Mary and her mother in the 1530s. Under these circumstances, Mary employed such experienced administrators, not because she trusted them, but because it remained impossible to conduct the business of government without them. Others, such as Rochester, Englefield, Waldegrave and Bedingfield, had seats on the Council because of their evident allegiance to the Catholic faith and because of their support for Mary in the crisis of her succession. Under such circumstances, forty-four men were sworn as royal councillors between July and October 1553.

The issue of the size of Mary's Council has been largely resolved by Dale Hoak's research. (9) Hoak's view is that 'the history of the formation of Mary's Privy Council is really the story of two Councils that became one'. Inexperienced, but reliably Catholic, councillors were recruited when Mary was effectively in revolt against Northumberland and 'Queen Jane'. These men were then upstaged when important members of Edward VI's Council came over to Mary. With the 'Catholic loyalists' relegated to positions that were more or less honorary, Hoak concluded, 'the resulting Privy Council functioned much in the manner of the ones appointed by Henry VIII, Edward VI and Elizabeth I'. The trend towards a 'select' Council, consisting of about a dozen skilled professionals, was reinforced by King Philip's preference for such a body.

The image of a divided Council owes much to the criticism relayed to the Emperor Charles V by his ambassador, Simon Renard. Renard was consistently keen to give his master the impression that Mary was ill-served by her Council and that it was only his own advice which promoted policies beneficial to Charles and to the Catholic Church. Renard's claims were largely accepted as fact by A.F. Pollard, who saw the two dominant figures of Mary's Council as representative of largely incompatible priorities. William, Lord Paget, was a flexible politician, well versed in the pragmatism of Henry VIII's reign, while Stephen Gardiner, Bishop of Winchester, was a conservative religious zealot, eager to see the reversal of many important aspects of the Henrician regime. Such an interpretation is open to question from several angles. Many writers have appreciated the selfish motives that may have guided Renard's self-advertisement. More recently, however, Ann Weikel (10) has suggested that it may be more accurate to see him, less as a scheming and biased diplomat with an agenda of his own than simply as a man whose appreciation of English politics was faulty, and whose judgement of English affairs was often simply unreliable. Similar judgements, after all, have been passed upon several of Philip II's ambassadors to England. David Loades (11) has also explored the problem in terms of contemporary mentalities. Spanish and Imperial diplomats would have had little experience of opinionated councillors, and it might well have appeared to them that these men 'ruled everything'. Mary's governmental inexperience, and her distrust of the men at her disposal, was probably paralleled by the fact that her councillors were the first in English history to work with a female monarch. 'Mary's councillors', writes Professor Loades, 'expected her to be irresolute and anxious to leave most of the business of government to them. To their surprise they found her obstinate beyond measure on issues of conscience.' At the same time, Dr Peter Donaldson (12) has argued that there may have been much more common ground between Paget and Gardiner than is often appreciated, with Gardiner much more of a pragmatist than Pollard supposed. Similarly, Ann Weikel's analysis of the grouping of councillors over specific political issues suggests that alliances were fluid and liable to change from one issue to another. She suggests that, unlike some of the great ministers of the Tudor period, neither Gardiner nor Paget was sufficiently charismatic, or possessed a sufficiently powerful political base, to command consistent loyalty and support. The disagreements that occurred within Mary's Council, therefore, were differences of political opinion rather than manifestations of genuine political factionalism.

Traditional criticisms of the business record of Mary's Council centred upon three main political issues; the Queen's marriage to Philip of Spain, the rebellion launched by Sir Thomas Wyatt in Kent early in 1554, and the restoration of Catholicism. Over two of these issues there were certainly important differences of opinion within the Council, and between the Queen and some of her councillors. Although Paget supported the Spanish marriage, other ministers sought to dissuade Mary from such a course when she finally communicated her prerogative decision to them in October 1553.

Equally, the parliamentary delegation which protested against the marriage in November was grouped around Gardiner and some of his conciliar allies, although the membership of the delegation cut across the supposed Gardiner/Paget lines. This, incidentally, provides us with an early example of councillors using the forum of Parliament to put pressure upon the monarch to depart from an unpopular course (compare Chapter 6). Once the royal course of action was irrevocably established, however, the Council did excellent work to ensure that it operated in the best interests of the monarch and of the realm. Gardiner and Paget worked closely together on the drafting of a marriage treaty which, by its close definition of Philip's status, its care for the commercial rights of Englishmen, and the implications of the marriage for the succession to the English throne provided adequate guarantees for England's continuing independence and prosperity. 'These terms were so favourable to England', Ann Weikel has concluded, 'that it is difficult to sustain the argument that they were achieved by an inefficient, faction-ridden council.'

Fundamental differences of opinion also existed within the Council on the subject of the restoration of Catholicism. In this case it was Gardiner whose views were more in tune with the Queen's, advocating a draconian response to heresy, while Paget hoped for a more sensitive restoration that would avoid social conflict and safeguard the interests of those who held former church lands. These differences resulted in the most serious example of governmental breakdown in the reign, when they spilled over into the parliamentary session of 1554. Gardiner's bill on religious measures was introduced in the Lords with Mary's approval, but without the knowledge of Paget and his supporters. Paget's parliamentary opposition led to confrontation with the monarch and to the councillor's temporary disgrace. It is hard to be critical of the Council's handling of Wyatt's rebellion without an uncritical acceptance of Renard's interpretation of events. The Council played a leading role in the detection of the wider plot of which the Kent rising was part. In the crisis conditions of January 1554 the councillors did much to prepare resistance in the capital to the rebels and, if the measures taken in Kent did not work (mainly due to the defection of some of Norfolk's troops), those taken in London were largely successful.

It is also important to remember that the duties of the Council extended beyond the formulation of 'grand policy' to the routine regulation of social and economic life. In these areas, although there is little evidence of Mary's personal interest, her councillors have an outstanding record. Although Professor Elton (13) saw the formation of conciliar committees as a retrograde step away from the Council's Cromwellian format, they did some excellent work. Eleven such bodies existed by February 1554, and many of the lesser councillors, who attended few Council meetings, served the crown effectively through the medium of these committees. Dr Loades concedes that 'the Marian system has an antique look about it, [yet] it worked because it was driven by a small team of dedicated and efficient royal servants'. Lord Treasurer Winchester rationalised financial administration in 1554 by annexing the Court of First Fruits and Tenths and the Court of Augmentations to the Exchequer. Another committee initiated (1555) a survey of crown lands and a revaluation of their rents, which resulted in an increase in income of some 40,000 pounds per annum. By similar means a new Book of Rates was introduced in May 1558 that tripled the crown's income from customs and excise dues. It was only because of the accident of the Queen's death that such reforms laid the bases for the prosperity and stability of Elizabeth's reign rather than that of Mary.

Such reasoning leads to two central conclusions. One is that the charges of factionalism and self-interest can only be sustained by exclusive concentration upon the relationship between Paget and Gardiner, a factor limited by Gardiner's early death (November 1555). If, on the other hand, one concentrates upon the achievements of such professional administrators as William Paulet, Marquis of Winchester, the charge of 'sterility' becomes a nonsense, and the work of the government appears as positive, productive and beneficial as that of any administration in the sixteenth century. The second conclusion is that, overall, Mary's experienced councillors performed well when left to their own devices. What is unusual about the reign in the development of Tudor government is less the quality of Mary's councillors and the advice that they provided, than Mary's reluctance to seek that advice. To a highly unusual degree the Queen formed and conducted her policies by prerogative decisions advised by men such as Renard and Pole, personal favourites rather than formal members of her government. It is in this, rather than in any other governmental sense, that the reign may truly be regarded as an aberration.

Questions

1. How acceptable is the view that the reign of Mary Tudor constituted a rare interlude of weak government in sixteenth-century England?
2. Did English government undergo a 'mid-Tudor crisis'?

SOURCES

1. THE DEVELOPMENT OF THE POST OF KING'S SECRETARY

Source A: from a letter from Richard Pace, the King's Secretary, to Cardinal Wolsey, written in 1518.

Please it your Grace this is to certify that this same hour I have received your Grace's letters dated the 17th of this present month with a packet directed unto the King's Highness which I shall immediately deliver unto his Grace after dinner. And where your Grace's pleasure is that I should move the King's Highness to read himself such letters as come out of Spain, your Grace shall understand that no letters be sent unto his Highness under your Grace's packet, but his Highness doth read them every word.

Source B: from a letter from Richard Pace, King's Secretary, to Cardinal Wolsey, 29 October 1521. Pace is replying to a complaint from Wolsey that he had communicated Wolsey's correspondence to the King inaccurately.

I never rehearsed your Grace's letters, diminutely or fully, but by the King's express commandment, who readeth all your letters with great diligence, and mine answers made to the same not by my device but by his instructions. And as for one of my letters, I had at that time devised a letter in the same matter far discrepant from that ye received; but the King would not approve the same, and commanded me to bring your said letters into his privy chamber, with pen and ink, and there he would declare unto me what I should write. So that I herein nothing did but obeyed the King's commandment as to my duty appertaineth.

Source C: from a letter by Eustace Chapuys, the Imperial ambassador, to the Imperial Chancellor, Granvelle, 1535.

Master Cromwell was a law-pleader, and thus became known to the Cardinal of York, who, perceiving his talents and industry, and finding him ready at all things, evil or good, took him into his service. On the Cardinal's downfall . . . Cromwell contrived with presents and entreaties to obtain an audience of the King, who he undertook to make the richest sovereign that ever reigned in England. He promised so fairly that the King at once retained him upon the Council. Since that time he has risen above everyone, except it be the lady, and the world says that he has more credit with his master than ever the Cardinal had. The Cardinal shared his influence with the Duke of Suffolk and several others. Now there is not a person who does anything except Cromwell.

Source D: from a letter to Thomas Cromwell from Sir Richard Grenville, writing from Cornwall, July 1539.

Notwithstanding at my being with your Lordship I showed you at that time that I would put your Lordship to no suit to the King's Majesty for me, neither for land nor for fee; but since I have bethought me that if I have not some piece of this suppressed land by purchase or gift of the King's Majesty I should stand out of the case of few men of worship in this realm. And because my heirs shall be in the same mind for their own profit, I will gladly, if it might stand with the King's Majesty's pleasure, buy certain parcels of the suppressed lands in these parts. The lands that I desire to have of the King's Highness be this: the priory of Launceston with the meadows and gardens, with a parcel of the demesnes called Newhouse, valued lately by the King's surveyors at fourteen pounds. Nor I do not do this for no covetousness but to stand in the case of others.

Source E: part of the royal warrant for the appointment of two Principal Secretaries, 1540.

First, that Thomas Wriothesley and Ralph Sadler shall have the name and office of the King's Majesty's Principal Secretaries during his Highness' pleasure; and shall receive, to be equally divided between them, all such fees, duties and commodities as have, do, or ought to belong to the office of his Majesty's Principal Secretary.

Item, his Highness hath resolved that every of the said Thomas Wriothesley and Ralph Sadler shall, for the time of their being in the said office, have and keep two of his Grace's seals, called his Signets; and with the same, seal all such things, warrants and writings, as have been accustomed to be passed heretofore by the same.

Item, his Majesty ordaineth that in all his councils, as well in his Majesty's household as in the Star Chamber and elsewhere, all lords, both of the temporalty and clergy, shall sit above them; and likewise the treasurer, comptroller, Master of the Horse, and Vicechamberlain of his Highness' household; then next after to be placed the said Principal Secretaries, and so, after them, all such other councillors as shall resort and have place in any of the said councils.

Questions

*1. Explain the following references that appear in the sources: 'the Cardinal of York' (Source C); 'he has risen above everyone, except it be the lady' (Source C); 'the suppressed lands in these parts' (Source D).

2. Sources A, B and D are all examples of correspondence

involving the King's Principal Secretary. What do you deduce from the tone and content of the sources about the changes in the status and role of the Secretary between 1518 and 1539?

3. What evidence is there in Source E to suggest that the post of Secretary diminished or increased in importance upon the fall of Thomas Cromwell in 1540?

4. 'The political influence of Thomas Cromwell owed little to the fact that he occupied the post of Principal Secretary.' To what extent is this statement supported by these sources or by other evidence known to you?

Worked answer

*1. [These questions simply test the student's background knowledge and comprehension, and should be answered as briefly as possible. At the same time the student should provide enough information to demonstrate awareness of any wider implications that the reference may contain.]

1 The reference here is to Thomas Wolsey, who held the office of Archbishop of York in addition to his status as Cardinal.

2 'The lady' is a reference to Anne Boleyn who, in the opinion of Chapuys, was the leading influence upon Henry at this time. He refers to her by this title because, given Charles's sympathy for Catherine of Aragon, it would have been unacceptable to refer to Anne as the Queen, or as Henry's wife.

3 The 'suppressed lands' refers to the lands formerly belonging to the monasteries. A proportion of these lands was sold through the Court of Augmentations to raise ready cash for the crown.

SOURCES

2. THE GOVERNMENT OF THE REALM UNDER MARY TUDOR

Source F: part of a petition submitted to Mary by Lord Paget and the Earl of Arundel at Framlingham, July 1553.

Our bounden duties most humbly remembered to your excellent Majesty. It may like the same to understand that we, your most humble, faithful and obedient subjects, having always, God we take to witness, remained your Highness's true and humble servants in our hearts, ever since the death of our late Sovereign Lord and master your Highness's brother, whom God pardon, and seeing hitherto no possibility to utter our determination without great destruction and bloodshed, both of ourselves and others, till this time, have this day proclaimed in your city of London your Majesty to be our true natural sovereign liege Lady and Queen; most humbly beseeching your Majesty to pardon and remit our former infirmities, and most graciously to accept our meanings, which have been ever to serve your Highness truly.

Source G: from a report by Giovanni Michieli, Venetian ambassador, to the Venetian Senate, 1555.

Respecting the government and public business, she is compelled (being of a sex which cannot becomingly take more than a moderate part in them) to refer many matters to her councillors and ministers. The truth is that, knowing the divisions which exist among them, her Majesty, in order not to be deceived and for the prevention of scandal, willed (with the King's consent) that Cardinal Pole should hear and have everything referred to him, it being evident that, whilst having the utmost confidence in him, she distrusts almost all the others.

Source H: extracts from letters written by the Imperial ambassador, Simon Renard, to the Emperor Charles V.

[February 1554] We talked with the Queen about the favours she might bestow on certain of her faithful subjects who had influence to win over others, in order to make friends for his Highness [Philip of Spain], and also to consider to whom some pension might be given.

Paget conferred with the Queen on the above point and sent us the names of the men who might have pensions. We did not definitely take Paget's advice, but thought it well to conciliate the others by talking over the matter with the Chancellor [Gardiner] and the Comptroller [Rochester], who have also given us a list of names in writing, with the sums appended, in accordance with which I have had 4,000 crowns melted down for [gold] chains, and the other 1,000 shall be distributed in money.

[14 November 1554] The limitation of the Council's membership is a somewhat invidious though necessary step, so the Queen herself had better decide to take it and let everyone realise that she has done so. It certainly seems that the Chancellor [Gardiner], Paget, the Bishop of Norwich [Thirlby], and Secretary Petre are experienced statesmen whose services are indispensable. As for the rest, they must be chosen in the light of knowledge of their characters. It would be a grave mistake to attempt to introduce any foreigners into the Council.

[23 November 1554] You may perhaps remember that I wrote some time ago with regard to the reduction of the excessive number of councillors. It has proved impossible to achieve this measure, for it created too much bad feeling between the old and recent members of the Privy Council, especially as the new list did not include the High Treasurer [Winchester], the Comptroller [Rochester], Walgrave [Sir Edward Waldegrave], the Lord Warden [Sir Thomas Cheyney], Englefield, and others who consider themselves to be as deserving as those who, as they say, rebelled against and resisted the Queen.

[10 February 1555] The split in the Council has increased rather than diminished; the two factions no longer consult together; some councillors transact no business; Paget, seeing that he is out of favour with the Queen and most of the Council, is often in the King's apartments.

Source I: notes on the meeting of the Privy Council on 23 February 1554, at which the Council appointed members to committees for the conduct of business.

The names of all such as be appointed for the purposes following:
To call in the debts and provide for money: my Lord Chancellor, my Lord Paget, my Lord Chamberlain, Mr Comptroller.
To give order for supply of all wants at Calais, Guisnes and other pieces in those Marches; to give like order for Berwick and other places upon the borders of the north; to give the like order for Ireland, Portsmouth, the Isle of Wight and the islands: my Lord Treasurer, my Lord Steward, my Lord Privy Seal, my Lord of Sussex, my Lord of Pembroke [and four others].
To consider what laws shall be established in this Parliament and to name men that shall make the books thereof: my Lord Chancellor, my Lord Treasurer, my Lord of Durham, my Lord Paget, Mr Petre, Mr Baker, Mr Hare.

Questions

1. Explain the following references that appear in these sources: 'Cardinal Pole' (Source G); 'those who, as they say, rebelled against and resisted the Queen' (Source H).
*2. In what respects does Source F help students of this period to understand Mary's relationship with her councillors? In what ways does it help to assess the validity of other sources that appear in this selection?
3. What considerations should the historian take into account in assessing the reliability of Simon Renard's correspondence as a source for the study of relations between Mary and her councillors?
4. On the strength of these sources, who appears to have

exercised the greatest influence upon the formulation of government policy during the reign of Mary Tudor?

5. 'Mary's English councillors played little part in either the formulation or the execution of government policy.' How far is this statement confirmed by these sources or by other evidence known to you?

Worked answer

*2. [This question requires the student to demonstrate an understanding of the historical context in which the document was produced, and then to consider other set sources and elements of background knowledge in the light of that understanding.]

The source illustrates the attempt of some of Edward VI's ministers to establish their loyalty to Mary at a time when Northumberland was still attempting to enforce the claims of Lady Jane Grey to the throne in Mary's place. It is important to appreciate that, essentially, the claims made by Paget and Arundel about their loyalty are untrue, and that they have only very recently distanced themselves from Northumberland and Jane Grey, possibly because they anticipated their failure. This petition, and the fact that Mary accepted it, helps the student to understand that Mary accepted the administrative talents of some of Edward VI's ministers, despite her awareness that they had not always been politically reliable. She was thus unlikely to place her full trust in them once she was safely placed upon the throne. This certainly helps to explain, and to substantiate, Michieli's statement in Source G that 'she distrusts almost all the others'. It also helps the student to understand why Renard consults Paget and Gardiner separately in Source H, and why he states in February 1555 that Paget was 'out of favour with the Queen'. Finally it helps to explain why, in November 1554, Renard should report that some councillors resent those of their colleagues who they perceive as having 'rebelled against and resisted the Queen'.

4

CENTRAL GOVERNMENT
Law and order

BACKGROUND NARRATIVE

Law, as the essential basis of social and political stability, was an obsessive concern for the governing and propertied classes of Tudor England. It might have been an exaggeration to claim, as the 1547 *Book of Homilies* did, that without such laws 'no man shall ride or go by the highway unrobbed, no man shall sleep in his own house or bed unkilled, no man shall keep his wife, children or possessions in quietness, all things shall be common'. Nevertheless, this represented the nightmare vision which the makers and enforcers of the law sought earnestly to avoid.

The governing assumption of English law was that the king dispensed justice personally to all subjects alike, and that his law was thus the 'common law' of the realm. As for centuries it had been impracticable for justice to be dispensed directly by the monarch and his Council, these functions had devolved upon two major common law courts. The Court of King's Bench exercised jurisdiction over cases concerning the rights of the crown and its subjects. Superior to other courts, it operated from a base in Westminster, and through a system of circuit judges, who toured the localities at fixed intervals, and held assize courts under the authority of a royal commission of oyer and terminer (Old French – 'to hear and to determine'). The Court of Common Pleas, on the other hand, heard cases between subject and subject. It sat at

Westminster and was by some margin the busiest, and therefore the slowest, of the Tudor law courts.

Yet such were the problems posed by time, distance and the sheer volume of legal business that there was still no comprehensive substitute for the personal, charismatic authority of the crown and its greatest ministers. The King's chief legal officer, the Lord Chancellor, therefore continued to play a central role in law enforcement. Sitting in the Court of Chancery, he heard cases that the common law courts had failed to determine satisfactorily. In doing so, he applied a system known as 'equity', effectively a process of natural justice and common sense, which sought to override difficulties and complexities in the common law, and to correct malfunctions in the lower courts. Increasingly the Exchequer expanded its capacity to hear common law cases which had financial implications. From 1585, indeed, the Court of Exchequer Chamber existed as a court of appeal from the Court of King's Bench in such cases.

During the fifteenth century the King's Council continued to play an active judicial role, separate from its political functions. Increasingly in the early sixteenth century these judicial functions were exercised by councillors sitting separately in the Star Chamber at Westminster, trying cases too difficult, or too politically sensitive, to be dealt with effectively in the lower courts. This so-called prerogative court took on greater significance under Wolsey and by 1540 operated as a distinct institution, even though its personnel continued to be drawn from the Council and the Chief Justices of the common law courts. At the same time, the development of the Court of Requests represented the extension of this 'conciliar' justice to deal with the suits of ordinary subjects, without the time, the money or the political muscle to succeed in other courts.

Routine law enforcement in the localities depended, however, upon a much less exalted body of officers. The Justices of the Peace were local gentlemen of substance commissioned by the crown (the Commission of the Peace) to enforce in their locality those statutes concerned with the maintenance of good order. They convened for this purpose four times a year in the so-called Quarter Sessions. Frequently criticised for their self-interest, and for their inability to enforce the interests of the crown against the vested interests of local magnates, the JPs nevertheless represented a valuable link and alliance between central government and local gentry. Their numbers increased steadily throughout the sixteenth century, as did the body of statute law that they were responsible for enforcing. By Elizabeth's reign it was certainly true that, in the words of Sir Thomas Smith, 'the Justices of the Peace be those in whom for the repressing of robbers, thieves and vagabonds, for riots and violences, and all other misdemeanours in the commonwealth, the prince putteth his special trust'.

In the early decades of the sixteenth century, this picture was considerably complicated by the survival of independent courts within the political franchises that existed in various parts of England and, of course, by the canon law courts of the Church. Such diversity was largely eliminated by a series of far-reaching reforms in the latter part of Henry VIII's reign. A comprehensive act of 1536 discontinued 'Certain Liberties and Franchises heretofore taken from the Crown', while other statutes (1536 and 1543) brought Wales into the legal framework of the English shires. No such reform, however, was possible in Ireland. In the process, of course, these reforms indicated the perceived superiority of parliamentary statute over even the most firmly established local, customary law. Canon law courts survived the dramatic reforms of the 1530s, yet they too were transformed in the sense that, subsequently, they were responsible to the crown as Supreme Head of the Church in England, and exercised the King's justice like any other court in the realm.

ANALYSIS (1): HOW EFFECTIVELY DID THOMAS WOLSEY FULFIL HIS DUTIES AS LORD CHANCELLOR OF ENGLAND?

Thomas Wolsey became Chancellor of England in December 1515, as part of his meteoric rise to power, and thus acquired responsibility for the enforcement and administration of secular law within the realm. His work in this office has been universally recognised as committed and energetic. Throughout fourteen years in the office, he spent several days a week during legal terms hearing cases in Chancery or in the Court of Star Chamber. Research has indicated that, in that time, he heard over 9,000 cases, 7,526 of them in Chancery (1) and 1,685 in Star Chamber. John Guy (2) has estimated that Wolsey's average of

120 cases per year in Star Chamber amounts to ten times the annual total recorded during Henry VII's reign. There can be no doubt that, under Wolsey's guidance, Star Chamber became a powerful weapon in the legal armoury of the crown.

A much greater degree of controversy has surrounded Wolsey's motives, methods and long-term effectiveness as Chancellor. The contemporary criticisms of John Skelton and of Polydore Vergil, both clients of Wolsey's political enemies, were echoed in the early twentieth century in the work of A.F. Pollard. (3) Such critics accused Wolsey of seizing greedily upon the office of Chancellor, the better to consolidate his personal political authority, and have accused him of exploiting the courts under his control to pursue vendettas against those who had earlier offended him. Other criticisms have been of a more serious constitutional nature; that by his extended use of equity and of the conciliar courts, Wolsey resisted and undermined the development of the common law. In this respect, as in others, Geoffrey Elton (4) drew unflattering comparisons with the next generation of Tudor ministers and, in particular, with Thomas Cromwell. Where Cromwell reformed Tudor government to an extent that Elton judged to be 'revolutionary', Wolsey persisted with the application of outmoded, late medieval legal forms. In Elton's judgement, 'Wolsey was a true amateur, eager to do the right thing, full of personal activity and driving energy, but unsystematic, lacking in direction and follow-through, and therefore ultimately sterile.'

The revision of Elton's interpretation of Cromwell's reforms in recent years has provided an opportunity for the reassessment of Wolsey's governmental and administrative achievement. John Guy and Peter Gwyn (5) have been in the forefront of this reassessment, reaching subtly different conclusions. Both have rejected the idea that Wolsey sought the office of Lord Chancellor for the power that it placed at his disposal. His predecessors in the office had not enjoyed such political dominance, and Thomas Cromwell enjoyed a similar degree of political influence without holding the office of Chancellor. Wolsey acquired legal authority for the same reason that he was given ecclesiastical and diplomatic functions, because Henry trusted him and wished him to apply his talents to a specific set of tasks, central to the interests of the crown. The illicit exploitation of local influence by powerful families and the maladministration of the common law in the localities were matters of great concern to Henry VIII as they had been to his father. John Guy maintains the view that Wolsey used this office as an advertisement for his own political authority. Peter Gwyn, however, depicts a minister concerned primarily to fulfil the King's wishes by maintaining order and applying the laws consistently. Such an interpretation easily acquits Wolsey of the charge that he took action against members of the nobility for reasons of personal vindictiveness, a charge which in any case is too obviously associated with contemporary factional propaganda to be credible today. Gwyn also rejects the charge that Wolsey deliberately obstructed the development and practice of common law. He notes how frequently common lawyers worked within the conciliar courts, and how regularly cases were referred back and forth between different courts.

Whatever his primary objective, there can be little doubt that in Chancery and Star Chamber, in John Guy's words, 'Wolsey investigated and attacked without delay the illegal acts, abuses and judicial malfeasance perpetrated in their counties by the King's own councillors'. The list of his 'victims' is especially impressive between 1516 and 1518, when the Earl of Northumberland, Lord Burgavenny, the Marquess of Dorset, Sir Andrew Windsor, Keeper of the Wardrobe, and Sir Robert Sheffield, former Speaker of the House of Commons, were all forced to appear before the Chancellor in Star Chamber. The appearance of Lord Burgavenny's name on this list reminds us that the problems of local order faced by Henry and his Chancellor were very similar to those confronted by Henry VII in the first decades of Tudor rule. At the same time Wolsey placed great pressure upon local officers to resist local magnate pressure and to follow the commands of central government. Justices of the Peace and sheriffs were ordered to London to renew their oaths of loyalty, and legal action was taken against specific individuals who were suspected of corruption. The effect was, in Diarmaid MacCulloch's (6) words, that 'Westminster had suddenly come very close to the lives of provincial rulers'.

Such a policy went hand in hand with the provision of quick and reliable justice for the King's poorer subjects, the very people most likely to be the victims of local malpractice. Contemporary critics pointed to the unmanageable workload that Wolsey created for himself in Star Chamber, but a direct 'spin off' from this was the establishment in Whitehall in 1519 of the judicial committee that developed into the Court of Poor Man's Requests. Peter Gwyn interprets the volume of business conducted by Wolsey in these years as an indication that Star Chamber and Chancery provided contemporary litigants with an option that they found more attractive than the common law courts. Closely linked to the issue of justice for the poor was the problem of enclosures. Although it remains unclear just how much responsibility Wolsey had for the anti-enclosure statutes of 1514 and 1515, it was he who established the commission that investigated the problem in

1517–18 and which led to 264 prosecutions in Chancery. J.J. Scarisbrick (7) is particularly impressed by the social status of those that Wolsey prosecuted in Chancery, noting that 'the list reads like a roll-call of the possessing classes of the Midlands'. The active presence of many of these 'victims' in the Parliament that attainted Wolsey in 1529–30 proves, in Scarisbrick's view, that the Chancellor's prosecutions hurt the guilty parties.

While it is hard to deny Wolsey's commitment to this policy of equitable justice, historians continue to argue that, in the long term, his work was ineffective. John Guy has commented that his 'idealism does not excuse his tendency to leave things half-finished'. Equally, he suggests that Wolsey failed to solve the major problems that he tackled. 'His impact on local government', Guy concludes, 'should not be exaggerated. If he aimed at centralised administration and a crown-controlled magistracy, the balance of power in the counties still remained with local landowners.' It is certainly true that the nature of Wolsey's position as the King's chief minister (see Chapter 2) forced him to change his priorities as Henry required, and application to legal business suffered when Henry's diplomacy or marital problems supervened. Similarly, in the 1523 Parliament, when money was the chief preoccupation, Wolsey was forced to compromise his anti-enclosure policy by granting an amnesty to offending landlords in return for their support for a subsidy. On the other hand, Peter Gwyn refutes the charge that his legal efforts were ultimately sterile with his own interpretation of the policy that Wolsey applied in his courts. Accepting that Wolsey's prosecutions only rarely led to serious punishment, Gwyn argues that this represented a necessary compromise in the context of the time. 'An appropriate punishment meant ensuring that [local magnates] were made fully aware that they were not above the law, but this did not usually mean that they were deprived of their role as leaders of their localities. The realities of the power structure in late medieval and early modern England imposed a certain degree of leniency and compromise upon the crown's and Wolsey's treatment of the powerful.' He further suggests that Wolsey's work in Chancery and in Star Chamber might reasonably be seen as part of Henry VIII's reaction to his father's 'terror tactics', as part of a 'return to normalcy' after the perceived excesses of Empson and Dudley.

A judgement upon Wolsey's efficacy as Chancellor depends largely upon the angle from which one examines his work. Seen in the context of later Tudor governments, with their greater degree of stability and centralisation, he may indeed appear amateurish and ineffective. Seen against the background of Henry VII's reign, however, and of the problems of law and government which his son inherited, Wolsey may reasonably be viewed as the most energetic and successful operator of the legal system of late medieval England.

Questions

1. To what extent does Cardinal Wolsey's record as Chancellor support G.R. Elton's judgement that he was a 'superb amateur in government'?
2. Compare the legal means by which the crown controlled the political elite during the reign of Henry VII and the first twenty years of the reign of Henry VIII.

ANALYSIS (2): WAS ENGLAND A MORE LAW-ABIDING COUNTRY AT THE END OF ELIZABETH'S REIGN THAN AT THE BEGINNING?

For much of the twentieth century the study of Tudor government has been approached from the angle of constitutional history. As historians have concentrated upon the development of governmental institutions and the laws that emerged from parliamentary sessions, a picture has emerged of an increasingly regulated and stable society in happy contrast to France or the Netherlands in the late sixteenth century. Yet such an approach makes it difficult to assess the realities of law enforcement, and in recent years the subject has increasingly been investigated by social historians, concentrating upon local records and seeking to assess the actual impact of the law upon social conduct and stability.

Studying Elizabethan law enforcement and law observance from the first of these angles, two things immediately become clear. Elizabethan England had more laws, and more people resorted to them for the solutions of their disputes. When a Kentish Justice of the Peace, William Lambarde, published a handbook for the guidance of his colleagues (1581–82), he listed 309 statutes which, in principle, JPs were obliged to enforce, and noted that 116 of them had become law since 1547. The accumulation of legislation continued after 1582 as the Poor Law was further elaborated and as JPs received extensive powers to take action against the impact of plague, grain shortages and similar problems. It is equally clear that the propertied classes turned increasingly to the law courts for the settlement of their disputes. Where the Courts of King's Bench and of Common Pleas heard about 2,600 cases per annum at the start of the 1560s, they were hearing 22,000 by the turn of the century. Similar increases are evident in other courts. The number of defamation cases heard in the consistory court of the Bishop of Chester, for instance, quadrupled between 1544 and 1594. While this trend cannot yet be comprehensively explained, Christopher Brooks (8) summarises the provisional conclusions, drawing attention to 'a cluster of social and economic changes – the increase in population and inflation, markedly greater activity in the land market, and the more extensive use of credit – which led to a remarkable growth in the amount of legal business that came before the courts'.

Elizabeth's reign certainly saw a dramatic decline in that form of illegal activity most dangerous to central government. Where the years between 1536 and 1554 had been punctuated by rebellions aimed at influencing the political, religious and economic policies of central government, only two such rebellions took place after 1558. One of these, the rebellion of the Earl of Essex in 1601, was an ill-judged attempt at a *coup d'état* by a desperate courtier. Far more dangerous was the so-called 'Revolt of the Northern Earls' in 1569. Yet while it certainly posed a serious challenge to the authority of William Cecil and other ministers, it constituted the last example of such localised, semi-feudal rebellion. Joyce Youings (9) provides what is now an orthodox interpretation in claiming that the northern magnates failed because 'the lack of support from their principal tenants demonstrated the growing anachronism of aristocratic territorial power in Elizabethan England'. Lawrence Stone (10) and Penry Williams (11) have elaborated upon this theme, arguing that as the gentry class and other property owners turned increasingly to the law courts, rather than to their weapons, to settle their differences, so they became less inclined to rally to the calls of discontented social superiors, and feudal revolt became a less viable political option.

If the prosperous were committing less crime, or, at least, less violent and treasonable crime, there is evidence that the poorer elements of society were proving harder to control in the latter years of the reign. These years provided extraordinary hardships for many of the population. The harvests of 1596 and 1597 were disastrous, and those of 1586, 1594 and 1595 were not much better. In addition, a decade and a half of warfare made its impact felt through taxation, the recruitment, passage and billeting of troops, and the many problems associated with their demobilisation and desertion. It is not easy for historians to reach definitive conclusions about levels of lawlessness based upon local records. Relatively few complete sets of court records have survived, and they are largely limited to the south-east of England. Nevertheless, work that has been carried out tends to suggest that crime figures increased as social conditions deteriorated, and many contemporaries were convinced that their society and their property were severely threatened by the 'many-headed multitude'. Working on the records of three south-eastern counties, J.S. Cockburn (12) has established that the incidence of violent crime was not alarmingly high, perhaps 1.6 indictments per 1,000 of the population in Hertfordshire throughout the reign, falling to 0.7 in Essex. Crimes against property, on the other hand, such as theft or attacks on enclosures, show a steady rise, with marked increases at times of poor harvests, particularly in the 1590s.

Two forms of crime were characteristic of the last Tudor decade. The first of these was localised rioting, usually centred on food supplies or enclosures. Food riots occurred in Ipswich and in Gloucester in 1586, and in Somerset, Kent and Sussex during the dearth years of 1596–97, while London saw repeated rioting in the 1590s, often directed against the city's government or against foreign artisans. Vagrancy, the other characteristic offence, was a crime in its own right, regardless of the vagrants' behaviour, but historians have disagreed about the extent of the problem and the social danger that it posed. A.L. Beier's (13) work on London suggests that this became a serious and largely insoluble problem in the economic climate of the 1590s. He traces 'a massive increase in London vagrancy between 1560 and 1625', and concludes that the city 'was experiencing large-scale juvenile delinquency'. John Pound, (14) however, is inclined to regard the capital as a special case, particularly attractive to criminals and to economic victims. Considering the country as a whole, he concludes that 'in normal circumstances both poverty and vagrancy were fairly well contained, and to say that either created a dangerous national situation would be to strain the evidence'.

If research has confirmed contemporary impressions that crimes against property were on the increase in the last years of Elizabeth's reign, historians largely reject contemporary fears that the government was about to lose control. Peter Clark's work on Kent (15) has highlighted the relatively small numbers of people involved in such disturbances, and their generally civilised behaviour. Although the Oxfordshire 'revolt' of 1596 had a more radical and violent agenda, only a dozen locals seem to have participated. Greatly as these events disturbed local officials, and the councillors to whom they reported them, many historians are willing to dismiss them as being, in A.G.R. Smith's (16) phrase, 'limited protests by small numbers of men and women against what they regarded as intolerable injustices'. Why, then, did the country not experience the kind of widespread popular unrest which had helped to topple Somerset's government in 1549? K. Wrightson (17) concludes that what had changed in fifty years was the attitude of the yeomanry and of other lesser property owners who, in the prosperity and stability of the preceding decades, had come to identify more closely with the social and political values of their social superiors:

> It was such men, the natural leaders of village society, whose support and leadership were vital if a large-scale rebellion were to get off the ground. But if they were increasingly regarding themselves as having a stake in the status quo, and if they were increasingly willing to differentiate themselves culturally from the poor, such support and leadership were much less likely to be forthcoming.

There can be little doubt that the 1590s formed a troubled conclusion to Elizabeth's long reign, and that her last years were regarded by many contemporaries as a period of stagnation, instability and danger. In legal and constitutional terms, however, they were proved wrong. The new dynasty inherited a governmental and legal structure that survived for some decades and which, in the final analysis, coped soundly with the difficulties of the last Tudor decade. The very fact that local notables were shocked and frightened probably contributed to their concerted effort to enforce the laws and to preserve the peace. As Joyce Youings has argued, with gentlemen and yeomen determined to preserve their stake in society, and increasingly involved in litigation to do so, 'the hedge-breaking and food riots of lesser folk, without effective leadership, were little more than a nuisance'. Law continued to perform its function in the last years of Elizabeth, not because its enforcement was outstandingly effective, but because, in matters of social order and stability, there was an impressive consensus among the propertied classes. The Elizabethan legal system, D.M. Palliser (18) concludes, 'should be judged by its own intention to control the people as a whole rather than to punish individual offenders; and judged by that standard it was reasonably successful'.

Questions

1. Does the reign of Elizabeth deserve its reputation as a 'golden age' of social prosperity and stability?

2. How similar were the problems of law enforcement faced by the governments of Henry VIII and Elizabeth?

SOURCES

1. WOLSEY'S EFFECTIVENESS IN THE LAW COURTS

Source A: an entry in the *Chronicle* of Edward Hall, dated 1516.

This year by the Cardinal were all men called to account that had the occupying of the King's money in the wars or elsewhere, not to every man's contentment; for some were found in arrears, and some saved themselves by policy and bribery and waxed rich, and some innocents were punished. And for a truth he so punished perjury with open punishment that in his time it was less used. He punished also lords, knights, and men of all sorts for riots, bearing and maintenance in their countries that the poor men lived quietly, so that no man durst bear for fear of imprisonment, but he himself and his servants were well punished therefore. The poor people perceived that he punished the rich, then they complained without number, and brought many an honest man to trouble and vexation. And when the Cardinal at the last had perceived their untrue surmises and feigned complaints for the most part, he then waxed weary of hearing their causes.

Source B: two verses about Wolsey by the satirical poet John Skelton. The first is from *Colin Clout*, published in 1522, and the second from *Why Come Ye Nat to Court?* published in 1523.

Men say how ye appall [i.e. detest]
The noble blood royal
Therefore ye keep them base,
And mock them to their face:
This is a piteous case,
To you that over the weal
Great lords must crouch and kneel
And break their hose at the knee,
As daily man may see.

In the Chamber of Stars
All matters there he mars,
Clapping his rod on the board.
No man dare speak a word,
For he hath all the saying

Without any renaying [i.e. contradiction].
He rolleth in his records,
He sayeth, 'How say ye, my lords?
Is not my reason good?'

Source C: letter from Thomas Wolsey to the King, written in 1517 or 1518.

And for your realm, Our Lord be thanked, it was never in such peace or tranquility; for all this summer I have had neither of riot, felony, nor forcible entry, but that your laws be in every place indifferently [fairly] ministered, without leaning in any manner. Albeit there hath lately been a fray between Pygot, your sergeant, and Sir Andrew Windsor's servants, for the seizure of a ward to which they both pretend titles, in the which fray one man was slain. I trust at the next term to teach them the law of Star Chamber. They be both learned in the temporal law, and I doubt not good example shall ensue to see them learn the new law of Star Chamber.

Source D: from a letter to Wolsey from the Bishop of Lincoln, 30 September 1528.

There was never thing done in England more for the Commonweal than to redress these enormous decays of towns and making of enclosures; for if your Grace did see as I have now seen, your heart would mourn to see the towns, villages, hamlets, manor places, in ruin and decay, the people gone, the ploughs laid down, the living of many honest husbandmen in one man's hand, the commons in many places taken away from the poor people. Never saw people so glad as they are now, hoping the King and Wolsey will see reformation made. They pray for the King and your Grace everywhere.

Source E: from a report by Sebastian Giustiani, Venetian ambassador, written in 1519.

The Cardinal is the person who rules both the King and the entire Kingdom. He is about 46, very handsome, learned, extremely eloquent, of vast ability and indefatigable. He, alone, transacts the same business as that which occupies all the magistracies, offices and councils of Venice, both civil and criminal, and all state affairs, likewise, are managed by him. He has the reputation of being extremely just: he favours the people exceedingly, and especially the poor; hearing their suits, and seeking to dispatch them instantly. He is of great repute – seven times more than if he were Pope.

Source F: from Polydore Vergil's *Anglica Historia*. This extract only appeared in the third edition of the work, published in 1555.

Acquiring so many offices at almost the same time, he became so proud that he began to regard himself as the equal of kings. Thus Wolsey, with his arrogance and ambition, roused against himself the hatred of the whole country, and by his hostility towards the nobility and the common people, caused them the greatest irritation through his vainglory. He was, indeed, detested by everyone because he assumed that he could undertake all the offices of state by himself. It was, indeed, a fine sight to watch this fellow, untrained in the law, sitting in court and giving judgement.

Questions

1. Explain the following references that occur in the sources: 'bearing and maintenance in their countries' (Source A); 'the commons in many places taken away from the poor people' (Source D); 'a ward to which they both pretend titles' (Source C).
2. In the light of Sources A and E, how reliable do you consider Polydore Vergil (Source F) to be as an historical source for this period?
*3. 'The poor people perceived that he punished the rich'. What different attitudes are displayed in Sources B, D and E towards Wolsey's apparent policy of protecting the poor against the rich? How might these different attitudes be explained?
4. How far do these sources lead you to believe that Chancery and Star Chamber were effective forms of law enforcement under Wolsey's chancellorship?

Worked answer

*3. [The question involves two different processes. The nominated sources must be examined, not simply for their content, but for the attitudes that lay behind that content. It is also necessary to examine the sources for evidence of bias, or of some form of vested interest. In some cases it may be possible to apply background knowledge to detect this interest. Otherwise it should be possible to deduce it through the application of common sense. These different processes may be carried out separately, and presented as different paragraphs, but it might make for a more fluent answer if the attitude and commitment of each source were dealt with together.]

Two of the nominated sources are extremely enthusiastic about Wolsey's legal sympathy for the King's poorer subjects. The Bishop of Lincoln (Source D) regards the Cardinal's measures against enclosures as being among the greatest services ever done 'for the Commonweal'. In rather more measured tones the Venetian ambassador (Source E) ascribes many outstanding qualities to Wolsey, and compliments his work in the law courts as being 'extremely just'. Of the two sources, we might take the ambassador's dispatch more seriously. It was the role of any ambassador to be objective, and to provide his masters with accurate information about the realm in which he was based. Even if we don't consider his conclusions to be accurate in all respects, for Wolsey did not necessarily 'rule the King and the entire Kingdom', we have no reason to believe that the account is biased. The Bishop of Lincoln responds to the problems of the poor as one might hope a leading cleric would do. On the other hand, he might find it hard to write anything but praise to the man who was not only the King's chief minister, but, as papal legate, his own ultimate superior within the English Church.

John Skelton's judgement in the first part of Source B goes to the opposite extreme. He appears to be outraged at Wolsey's treatment of the nobility, who must 'crouch and kneel' before the upstart minister. Background knowledge tells us that Skelton was a client of the Duke of Norfolk, a major political rival of Wolsey, but even without this knowledge, one might conclude that he mistrusted the Cardinal's legal procedures as a dangerous attack upon the established social order.

On balance, therefore, two of the three sources have some degree of vested interest behind their judgement on Wolsey's apparent policy of 'punishing the rich'. Only the Venetian ambassador provides a judgement that is not suspect in some way, and he portrays the minister's policy in a most positive light.

SOURCES

2. THE EFFECTIVENESS OF ELIZABETHAN JUSTICES OF THE PEACE IN LOCAL LAW ENFORCEMENT

Source G: from Sir Thomas Smith's treatise on English government, *De Republica Anglorum*, written in 1583.

The justices of the peace be those in whom at this time for the repressing of robbers, thieves and vagabonds, of privy complots and conspiracies, of riots and violences, the prince putteth his special trust.

And commonly every year or each second year in the beginning of summer (for in the warm time the people for the most part be more unruly, even in the calm time of peace) the prince with his Council chooseth out certain articles out of the penal laws already made for to repress the pride and evil rule of the popular and sendeth them down to the justices. And then within certain space they meet again and certify the prince or his Privy Council how they do find the shire in rule and order touching those points and all other disorders. There was never in any commonwealth devised a more wise, a more dulce [sweet] and gentle, nor a more certain way to rule the people, whereby they are kept always as it were in a bridle of good order, and sooner looked unto that they should not offend than punished when they have offended.

Source H: two pieces written by William Lambarde, a Kent JP, and author of *Eirenarcha*, a guide to the office of JP.

From a speech made at the Kent Quarter Sessions in 1586.

It must be confessed that this, as all other wars, will bring the wonted evils and companions of war and hostility with it. For now such men as have more valour in their bodies than virtue in their minds will think that all the labour lieth on their hands and will therefore grow insolent and boldly adventure on the breach of the laws in hope that they may not only escape punishment but pass without controlment of it. Now will your sons and servants strive to draw their necks out of the yoke of due obedience. Now will beastly drunkards and blasphemers vaunt that they be valiant and serviceable men.

From an address delivered at Maidstone, 17 January 1594.

That the number of our people is multiplied, it is both demonstrable to the eye and evident in reason, considering on the one side that nowadays not only young folks of all sorts, but churchmen also of each degree do marry and multiply at liberty, which was not wont to be, and on the other side that we have not, God be thanked, been touched with any extreme mortality, either by sword or sickness, that might abate the overgrown number of us.

Lastly, the poor are exceedingly much multiplied because for the most part all the whole children and brood of the poor be poor also, seeing that they are not taken from their wandering parents and brought up to honest labour for their living but, following their idle steps, so they do live and die, most shameless and shameful rogues and beggars.

Source I: part of a letter written to Lord Burghley by Edward Hext, a Justice of the Peace in Somerset, 25 September 1596.

I know that in the experience of my service here, that the fifth person that committeth a felony is not brought to this trial, if they be taken and come unto the hands of the simple man that hath lost his goods, because he will not be bound to give evidence at the assize to his trouble and charge. Others are delivered to simple constables that sometimes willfully, other times negligently, suffer them to escape. Others are brought before some Justice that either wanteth [lacks] experience to examine a cunning thief or will not take the pains that ought to be taken in sifting him upon every circumstance and presumption. In default of justice many wicked thieves escape, for most commonly the simple countryman and woman, looking no further than unto the loss of their own goods, are of opinion that they would not procure a man's death for all the goods in the world. And these that thus escape infect great numbers, emboldening them by their escapes, some having their books by the entreaty of the justice themselves that cannot read a word, others having been burned in the hand more than once, for after a month or two there will be no sign in the world. And the greatest part are now grown to these petty felonies for which they may have their book, by which they are emboldened to this great wickedness.

Source J: from a letter written by Edwin Sandys, Archbishop of York, to Lord Burghley, 1587.

I have noted in a paper, herein enclosed, such as in my opinion may be well put out of the commission [i.e. dismissed as Justices of the Peace]. I deal with no knights, lest I should be noted to follow affection; but I assure you some of them be of the baddest sort, unworthy to govern, being so far out of order themselves. And to speak the truth, although there be many gentlemen in Yorkshire, yet it is very hard to choose fit men for that purpose.

Robert Lee. He is a notable open adulterer, one that giveth offence and will not be reformed. He useth his authority as well to work private displeasure as to serve other men's turns.

Peter Stanley. A man noted to be a great fornicator. Of small wisdom, and less skill.

Thomas Wentworth. A very senseless blockhead, ever wronging his poor neighbours. He bought grain in the beginning of last year in every market, and heaped it up in his houses to sell at the dearest.

Francis Alford. This man liveth much in London. A man of small living, less skill and no countenance.

Questions

1. Explain the following phrases that occur in Edward Hext's letter (Source I): 'a felony'; 'some having their books . . . that cannot read a word'; 'having been burned in the hand more than once'.
2. Compare the explanations put forward by William Lambarde (Source H) and by Edward Hext (Source I) for the disorder and the law-enforcement difficulties of the 1590s.
3. Compare the criticisms of JPs and their weaknesses that are put forward in Source I and in Source J.
*4. 'There was never in any commonwealth . . . a more certain way to rule the people.' To what extent do the other sources, and any other evidence known to you, lead you to consider that Sir Thomas Smith's verdict on the Justices of the Peace (Source G) was too optimistic?

Worked answer

*4. [On the face of it, this is a large and demanding question, but in the context of a documentary exercise it must be answered concisely. Half of the answer should consist of a summary of the evidence derived from the sources about the effectiveness of the JPs and the system of which they were part. A roughly equal space should then be devoted to a brief selection of evidence from the student's background knowledge dealing with the same issues.]

In considering the evidence contained in the sources themselves there are two issues to resolve, one concerned with the quality of the JPs and the other with their collective ability to contain disorder and lawlessness in their localities. In Source J, Archbishop Sandys makes a series of scathing judgements upon some of the JPs that he has encountered in Yorkshire, and draws the broader conclusion that 'it is very hard to choose fit men for that purpose'. Nevertheless, Sandys deals mainly with the moral character of the JPs, rather than with their effectiveness in their office, and we have no conclusive evidence that these men did not maintain law and order in their localities. William Lambarde (Source H) and Edward Hext (Source I) certainly appear to be men of greater quality than those described by Sandys. The one analyses the problems that he is facing with considerable thought and insight, while the other reports in detail to the government, in just the way that Sir Thomas Smith describes in Source G. Hext's letter, however, has several different sides to it. On the one hand, it is the work of a thorough and conscientious JP. On the other, it describes a system that the writer considers deficient, and even on the point of collapse.

Background knowledge of the period demonstrates, in fact, that Hext was overreacting to a degree. The socio-economic crisis of the 1590s did not lead to the collapse either of the system of local law enforcement, or of society in general. The authorities were able to deal effectively with disturbances in Kent, Oxfordshire and elsewhere. It is also evident, from the substantial and increasing workload that the government placed upon the JPs, that it had considerable confidence in the system. Sir Thomas Smith's judgement is drawn from a treatise on the government of contemporary England, and it is likely that he is drawing comparisons, not actually with 'any commonwealth', but more specifically with the earlier experience of Tudor England. His frame of reference would embrace the extensive local disorder of the early years of Tudor power, and the dramatic social unrest of 1549. For all its faults, the system that he describes would appear more effective and less dangerous to the interests of the governing classes than what had gone before.

5

THE GOVERNMENT OF THE LOCALITIES

BACKGROUND NARRATIVE

The vast majority of English men and women in the sixteenth century rarely came into contact with central government. For them, the effectiveness of Tudor rule depended upon the effectiveness of local government. Much of the minutiae of local affairs was of limited interest to central government and was handled throughout this period by a host of ancient and truly local bodies, such as the manor court, the court leet, and the institutions of the parish. In more important matters, such as defence, taxation or law enforcement, the crown became increasingly eager to exert its influence in the localities, and the means by which it sought to do so underwent significant change in the course of the sixteenth century.

In the English shires, the archetypal agents of Tudor authority fell into two categories. In the first of these were the great magnates, effective by virtue of their great estates and local prestige. For all the dangers of magnate power, the early Tudors could not easily do without it. Instead they sought to guarantee that it would be exercised in the name and in the interests of the crown. Thus, while Henry VIII's reign saw the steady elimination of political franchises, such as Durham or Chester, in which the local lord was effectively more powerful than the King, the crown continued to make very wide use of more reliable courtier-nobles. Such men as the Howards, Dukes of Norfolk, the Talbots, Earls of Shrewsbury and

Charles Brandon, Duke of Suffolk, played important roles in the first half of the century in enforcing royal authority in many parts of the realm. This trend began to be formalised in the mid-century in the increasing importance of the office of Lord Lieutenant. This office had its origins in the commissions issued by Henry VIII (1512, 1536 and 1545) to organise defence against Scottish and French aggression, and resistance to the Pilgrimage of Grace. Similarly, Northumberland sent lieutenants into several counties in the aftermath of the 1549 risings. Between 1585 and 1587, when England was threatened with Spanish invasion, Lords Lieutenant were appointed for most English counties, and the office became an essential link between central and local government. The post was usually entrusted to great officers of state, although the holder invariably relied upon the support of a local team drawn from the gentry of the shire. Inevitably, it was these local officers, particularly the Deputy Lieutenant, who carried most of the workload. Predominantly concerned with military matters at first, the Lords Lieutenant and their teams acquired many other duties, such as the administration of taxation, and the enforcement of religious conformity and economic legislation.

The second category of royal agents in the localities consisted of those directly appointed by the crown, whose prestige derived from the authority of this royal commission. Traditionally the most prominent royal official in each of the shires was the Sheriff. His duties were predominantly legal, such as the empanelling of juries and the execution of legal sentences, but they were also entrusted with such tasks as tax collection and combating religious dissent. The Sheriffs, however, had often provided insufficient protection for royal interests during the instability of the fifteenth century, and the office was generally in decline. This decline was offset in Tudor local government by the development of the office of Justice of the Peace (see Chapter 4). The effectiveness of such officials remains uncertain. The steady increase in their number and the enormous increase in their workload suggest that the crown regarded them as important agents. On the other hand, the constant chivying that they received from the Privy Council and the occasional purging of their ranks suggest that they did not always live up to this billing. Apart from such permanent officers, the crown might also make its will felt in the localities by means of teams of agents, commissioned temporarily to fulfil specific functions. The most important of these in the Tudor period were the commissions established to oversee the dissolution of the monasteries under Henry VIII, to inquire into enclosures on the authority of Protector Somerset, and to investigate Catholic recusancy during Elizabeth's reign. In addition, of course, the English localities were linked to central government by a common system of law enforcement (see Chapter 4), and by representation in Parliament (see Chapter 6).

It was particularly difficult to enforce royal authority in the distant corners of the realm. In the far north of England and in the Welsh marches, the Tudors had to rely either upon the magnates whose patronage and kinship networks dominated the area, or upon regional councils, controlled and directed by reliable courtiers. Between the accession of Henry VII and the mid-1520s, the crown had little option but to rely upon the great families of the north, the Percies, the Nevilles and the Dacres, for the maintenance of law and order, and for the defence of the borders against the Scots. Subsequently, however, the Council of the North steadily became a more viable alternative, particularly in the aftermath of successive failed rebellions of 1536 and 1569. By 1572, when the Earl of Huntingdon, the Queen's cousin, presided over the Council, its competence embraced trade, industry, poor relief, religious conformity, parliamentary elections, and much more. Wales shared many of the administrative problems of northern England, in terms of distance and difficult terrain, but it had no such magnates as the Percies and did not border on a hostile kingdom. Although a Council of the Marches fulfilled important legal functions in this locality in Henry VII's and in the first half of Henry VIII's reign, it was a much easier matter to assimilate Wales into the English pattern. In 1536 an Act of Union dissolved the marcher lordships, created five new counties, and introduced an English pattern of administration with JPs and parliamentary representation.

In one sense it is misleading to treat Ireland as an English 'locality', for the problems that it presented were atypical and particularly complex. The English king was, until 1541, merely 'lord' of Ireland, and after that date ruled Ireland in theory as a separate kingdom. He ruled through a Lord Deputy, seated in Dublin, and assisted by a Chancellor, a Council and the Chief Justices of two legal benches. The Lord Deputy also had the authority to summon a separate Irish Parliament. In practice, however, part of Ireland at least was administered in much the same way as any English locality. The Pale, the area around Dublin, which had experienced the earliest and most firmly established English settlement, was divided into counties and governed by the English common law. To the west and south-west of the Pale, the 'obedient lands' consisted of a mixture of shires and feudal lordships in the hands of Anglo-Irish nobles. The towns within these areas were English outposts, often bolstered in that capacity by extensive grants of liberties from the English crown. Roughly two-thirds of Ireland, however, was completely beyond English influence, in the hands of a variety of Gaelic chieftains, each exercising authority through his own tribal customs and laws.

ANALYSIS (1): HOW EFFECTIVELY WAS THE ENGLISH CROWN ABLE TO GOVERN IRELAND IN THE REIGNS OF THE FIRST TWO TUDORS?

Tudor rule in Ireland has usually been studied in a very different manner from other aspects of Tudor administration. For most historians studying the government of Tudor England, Ireland provides a foot-note, a territory in which the broad political aims of the crown were undermined by distance and by local vested interests. In the course of its 500 pages, G.R. Elton's classic work, *The Tudor Constitution*, makes only three references to Ireland. Irish historians have devoted much more energy to the subject, but have often worked with a distinct agenda of their own. Focusing upon the eventual independence of the country, they have often been content to view Tudor policy towards Ireland as primarily 'colonial', and have frequently described contemporary political developments mainly in the context of Irish resistance to English political influence.

In recent years Steven Ellis (1) has made two far-reaching, revisionist claims, one relating primarily to Irish history, and one with much wider implications for the subject of Tudor government. In the Irish context, he has rejected the notion that the magnates who dominated Irish government at this time, such as the Earls of Kildare, should be seen as the precursors of a 'home rule' movement, resisting the influence of the English crown. Such interpretations 'run counter to the most basic understanding of Tudor politics', for 'the early Tudors were no more likely to appoint an Irishman as governor of Ireland than a Frenchman as governor of Calais'. Such men, he contends, were typical elements of the English nobility, distinct only in terms of their remoteness from the seat of government. In the wider context, Professor Ellis stresses that Kildare's relative independence was by no means unique. Drawing close parallels between this 'Kildare ascendancy' and the 'Dacre ascendancy' in the far north of England, he concludes that such enforced reliance upon distant and semi-reliable magnates was a much more common feature of early Tudor administration than many constitutional historians have been willing to admit. These have been far too ready to judge the efficacy of Tudor government by its successes in southern England, and to neglect the distant marches, where the crown's writ did not automatically run and where effective government did not always take place. 'The society and economy of the early-Tudor north and Ireland were perhaps in many ways more typical of the British Isles in 1500 than was the south-east which forms the traditional focus of Tudor historical attention.'

The Earls of Kildare (2) were central to the English government of Ireland between the 1470s and the 1530s, and any assessment of its success depends very largely upon one's interpretation of their roles and priorities. Edmund Curtis (3) spoke for many Irish historians when he described the 8th Earl as 'All-but-King of Ireland, who stood for Home Rule against English interference'. Kildare, Curtis claims, 'could have destroyed England's petty forces in Ireland and made himself king'. A more traditionally English approach has been to view Kildare as the 'overmighty subject' *par excellence*, his local clientage and prestige making it impossible for the crown to bring him to heel. Professor Chrimes (4) reflects this interpretation in describing him as 'the most powerful man in Ireland, the man whom Henry himself could not subdue and therefore after years of contention found he could not do without'. Both interpretations reflect badly upon Henry VII's government of Ireland, suggesting that Kildare's feudal subordination to Henry was little more than fictional. In Professor Ellis's view, however, Kildare was not an 'overmighty subject' tolerated by a King who could not control him. He and Dacre alike should be seen as 'lesser nobles who were built up, with the active support of the early Tudors, into great territorial magnates' as a more safe and effective way of governing distant territories. The alternative, to entrust power to substantial English noblemen, backed with substantial financial support from the English Exchequer, was, in the context of the Wars of the Roses, a much more risky policy. English kings now 'groped towards some kind of response which combined the effective devolution of authority with the retention of overall central control. In Ireland the response was the maintenance of a complete but dependent administration, modelled on that for England, under the control of a viceroy.'

It is equally important to establish whether 'the great Earl' served the interests of the English crown in Ireland, and whether he could be effectively controlled by central government. Henry VII's Irish ambitions were strictly limited. He sought to ensure that the political leaders of the Anglo-Irish population acknowledged the new dynasty and did not allow their territories to serve as a base for pretenders. Beyond that he sought good government within the Pale and its security against the raids of Gaelic chieftains. Kildare's association with Lambert Simnel in the early years of the reign showed clearly that his reliability could not be taken for granted, but the mission of Sir Edward Poynings as Lord Deputy between 1492 and 1496 did a great deal to consolidate the authority of the crown. Its aim, as defined by Professor Chrimes, was 'to end the Wars of the Roses in Ireland as in England. It was the utmost that he could achieve or aspire to do, and by and large, this is what he did.' The package of reforms imposed by Poynings deprived the Lord Deputy of the powers to alienate royal lands, to grant pardons without direct royal consent, and to summon the Irish Parliament without specific approval from the English crown. Professor Loades (5) is equally convinced that these reforms created a situation in which Kildare could be trusted and controlled in his government of Ireland, and that subsequently he 'governed Ireland through a contractual understanding with the King, which enabled him to retain most of the profits and patronage of his office in return for his services'.

Subsequently, Kildare's 'track record' was very sound. Compared with the northern English marches, which were twice faced with full-scale Scottish invasion in Henry VIII's reign, as Ellis says, 'the Pale suffered no worse indignity than constant border raiding'. Kildare was an energetic Lord Deputy, extending his influence in Gaelic Ireland both by vigorous campaigns against the Gaelic chieftains in 1498, 1499, 1503, 1504 and 1510, and by marriage alliances. He established good relations with many of the Gaelic chieftains and built up a clientage that stretched well beyond the Pale. No doubt, as a number of Irish historians (6) have argued, this blurred and reduced the distinction between Anglo-Irish and Gaelic elements in Irish society, and no doubt Kildare did this largely in his own interests. Yet the security of the Pale was an agreeable by-product, and such factors as growing rent returns and attendance figures for Parliament suggest that these were years of relative prosperity and stability within the Pale. Viewing the issue from the angle of the English government, Steven Ellis seems to be justified in his conclusion that 'in so far as the problem of governing a distant border province a fortnight's journey away from the centre of power was soluble in this age of personal monarchy, Henry VII had solved his Irish problem'.

Although the early stages of Henry VIII's reign saw no significant changes in the way that Ireland was governed, the 'Kildare ascendancy' began to crumble in the course of the 1520s. The reasons for this were complex. Historians of Irish independence have emphasised the 9th Earl's increasingly close links with Gaelic chieftains and their culture, and have interpreted these as evidence of his declining loyalty to the Tudors. Others have linked his fall more closely to political developments in England, noting the involvement of Kildare and the rival Butler family with the English factional struggles associated with the rise of the Boleyn family. G.R. Elton, (7) unsurprisingly, linked Kildare's decline to the ascendancy of Thomas Cromwell and his broader plans for the extension of the crown's central, administrative control. Cromwell's policy, he claims, 'was visible from the first. He meant to end the independence of the feudal earldoms, to reform the government of the obedient parts, and to adopt for the time being an attitude of disengagement from the "disobedient" Irishry.' It is also probable that Henry VIII's dramatic break from Rome left the English crown in a more isolated position than it had known since the early years of Henry VII's reign, and greatly increased the government's concern with the security of Ireland.

Whatever the reasons, Kildare's authority finally collapsed in the dramatic rising of 1534 when, with the 9th Earl imprisoned in the Tower on spurious charges of treason, his son, 'Silken Thomas', responded with actions that were undeniably treasonable. His condemnation of Henry's religious policy, his renunciation of the crown's authority, and his attempts to raise Ireland in revolt, were met by determined English action. His defeat, arraignment and execution for treason (1537) not only ended the 'Kildare ascendancy' in Ireland, but demonstrated that for some years it had rested upon a delicate basis of Tudor sufferance.

The collapse of Kildare's power forced Henry VIII and his ministers to find other means of governing Ireland, and they took radical steps to bring Ireland more closely into line with English governmental practice. Where Cromwell had been content with governmental reform within the Pale, Henry assumed the title 'King of Ireland' (1541) and sought to revolutionise his political relationship with the Gaelic chieftains through the policy of 'surrender and re-grant'. The chieftains were invited to surrender their traditional authority in return for English titles directly granted by the crown. By so doing, they now acknowledged that they held their lands directly from the crown, and accepted the use of

English law and customs in their lands. Substantial as such changes were in theory, however, this was, as Grenfell Morton (8) described it, merely a 'legal framework whose reality was to be slowly filled in under Elizabeth and James I'. The reality of Henry's authority over Ireland in the 1540s may be gauged by the fate of the English reformation legislation, introduced into Ireland in 1536. The dissolution of the monasteries proved to be largely inoperable outside the Pale, and the first Jesuit mission appeared in Ireland in 1542, over thirty years before anything of the kind was launched in England. 'Of the Bishops in office at the passing of the Reformation legislation,' R.D. Edwards (9) has concluded, 'six (or at most eight) accepted the new spiritual allegiance, while twenty-one continued in communion with Rome.'

It is tempting to conclude that Ireland represented the greatest failure of Henry VIII's attempts to extend his own central power, and that in Ireland the 'revolution in government' worked in reverse. Governors, whose authority consisted of royal patents, rather than of local patronage and interests, actually reduced, rather than increased, royal authority. The more informal methods of Henry VII fitted the circumstances better, and ensured that between the late 1490s and the late 1520s, Ireland posed no significant difficulties for the Tudor monarchy. The formalisation of the 1540s destroyed that balance and, however convincing it may have seemed on paper, largely confirmed that the methods applicable in 'lowland' England were not suitable for outlying regions such as Ireland. 'Tudor Ireland gradually ceased to be governed by the normal methods of English administration,' writes Steven Ellis, 'and was subjected to military conquest, colonisation, and expropriation of the natives, with results which remain apparent down to the present.'

Questions

1. What justification is there for the view that the English crown failed to control the Earls of Kildare between 1485 and 1530?
2. Summarise the major difficulties faced by the English crown in the reigns of Henry VII and Henry VIII in its attempts to govern Ireland.

ANALYSIS (2): WITH WHAT SUCCESS DID TUDOR GOVERNMENTS IN THE SECOND HALF OF THE SIXTEENTH CENTURY TACKLE SOCIAL AND ECONOMIC PROBLEMS IN THE LOCALITIES?

The study of the Tudor economy, and of the impact of government legislation upon it, has a much shorter history than the study of Tudor politics or religion. Only in the latter part of the nineteenth century did economic and social historians begin a systematic investigation of the attitudes of central government towards local problems of trade, living standards and poverty. Their work established one of the most durable concepts associated with sixteenth-century government, that of 'Tudor paternalism'. They perceived Tudor governments as increasingly concerned with the regulation of economic and social life, and increasingly eager to intervene to protect or to enhance the living conditions of the populace at large. Professor F.J. Fisher (10) provided a good summary of this viewpoint with his claim that, from the 1550s and 1560s, Tudor governments made a coherent attempt 'to mould the economic system according to something like a pattern: the opening of distant markets and the organisation of those already in existence, the encouragement of new industries and the control of production in the old, the regulation of the whole pace of economic change and the public provision for the unemployed'.

Although such writers appreciated Wolsey's anti-enclosure measures (see Chapter 4) and the apparently enlightened social policies of the Duke of Somerset (see Chapter 1), they were particularly impressed by the volume of legislation passed in the second half of the sixteenth century. Such legislation addressed a very wide range of social and economic problems. Some statutes sought to maintain standards of industrial production, particularly in the manufacture of woollen cloth (1552), but also in the production of less important items such as pins (1543), linen (1559) and wax (1581). Other legislation dealt with such economic malpractice as forestalling and engrossing (that is, cornering supplies of scarce commodities and forcing up prices). The famous Statute of Artificers of 1563 sought to regulate a wide range of issues relating to agricultural employment, wage levels and apprenticeship. Above all, Elizabeth's reign saw a succession of Poor Laws that confirmed the distinction between those who could not and would not work, and introduced a compulsory poor rate with the parish as the local administrative unit. Relatively recently, Peter Ramsey (11) could still conclude that the Elizabethan poor-relief legislation as a whole 'offers perhaps the best evidence of Tudor paternalism in action, and the increased readiness of the state to intervene in social life'.

The concept of 'Tudor paternalism' has been modified by later writers in three important respects. Many of these later authorities have taken the view that the motives behind Tudor legislation were not primarily economic. Local order and stability were the major priorities for the government, with considerations of financial gain not far behind. For that reason many of the most important bursts of legislation follow on the heels of severe economic depression or periods of social unrest. The acts of 1552 regulating standards in cloth production and condemning forestalling and engrossing sought to restore confidence in the wake of the 'mid-Tudor' commercial crisis. In particular the substantial legislation of the 1590s was associated with the widespread fear that the social order was threatened by the vagrants and criminals who emerged from the serious economic crisis of that decade. Seen in this light, late Tudor legislation may be interpreted more as a series of panic reactions than as evidence of a coherent philosophy of government intervention.

Secondly, it is now widely recognised that the initiative for socio-economic legislation did not often come from central government. In the case of poor relief, in particular, parliamentary legislation was preceded by a number of sophisticated local initiatives. Research into Tudor urban history has revealed advanced systems of relief in Ipswich (from 1557), Norwich (from 1570), York, Cambridge and Exeter. London itself introduced a compulsory assessed poor rate as early as 1547 and contained at least three major hospitals established for the relief of the 'impotent' poor, along with Bridewell Prison for the punishment of vagabonds. John Pound (12) has stressed that the 1563 Poor Law was largely inspired by such precedents, and that once London, Norwich and Ipswich had established compulsory poor rates, 'the central authorities tentatively followed suit'. Even then, Sir John Neale (13) insisted in his outstanding study of Elizabeth's Parliaments that the bulk of the legislation on poor relief was not the work of central government, but of the Commons MPs themselves. At about the same time Professor Bindoff (14) was making similar claims about the Statute of Artificers. Although that measure originated with the government, he concluded, it was widely amended in the Commons by MPs with strong local, economic and social interests to cover areas, such as apprenticeship, with which the government had not initially been greatly concerned. By no means, therefore, should it be seen as evidence of far-seeing and comprehensive economic statesmanship on the part of Elizabeth's ministers.

The third area in which the concept of 'Tudor paternalism' has been questioned is in terms of the legislation's implementation and effectiveness. Some years ago an outstanding survey by the American historian W.K. Jordan (15) suggested that local authorities rarely levied the poor rate other than in times of economic emergency, and that central government made no sustained effort to enforce the Poor Laws until the 1630s. Jordan also produced figures to suggest that private charities continued to be a much more effective means of relieving the poor than the rate imposed by the government. He claimed that between 1560 and 1600 little more than 12,000 pounds was paid out of local taxation towards poor relief, while as much as 174,000 pounds was given for the same purposes out of private charities. Paul Slack (16) has gone further, claiming not only that parliamentary legislation achieved relatively little, but that local initiatives barely scratched the surface of the problem: 'In practice little was done before 1603. Although some of the larger towns had houses of correction, workhouses, or work stocks, they were always small, they rarely lasted long, and they were often mismanaged.' M.G. Davies (17) drew broadly similar conclusions about the effectiveness of the Statute of Artificers, concluding that the prescribed seven-year period of apprenticeship 'was neglected by central and local government, with rare exceptions, throughout the eighty years before the Civil War'. Although local self-interest undoubtedly played a major role in such neglect, there is also some evidence of local resistance to taxation and poor rates on the grounds that they ran contrary to more traditional, neighbourly methods of relieving the poor of the local community. It was sometimes felt, in the words of one Yorkshire petition against the poor rate, that 'many are able to give relief which are not able to give money'.

For all these modifications, many historians still regard the notion of Tudor state paternalism as valid, and in some senses it has enjoyed a revival in recent years. Paul Slack reminds us that the government did not only act through parliamentary statutes, but used a range of other means to deal with socio-economic problems in the localities. In particular he draws attention to the Books of Orders that the Council circulated to JPs, with instructions relating to plague conditions (first circulated in 1578) and to harvest failure and grain shortages (first circulated in 1586). Although no statute existed on the subject of plague until 1604, such orders were widely circulated and obeyed, especially in the very difficult years of the late 1580s and the 1590s. Recent writers have tended once more to take a positive view of the impact of Tudor social legislation. While they accept that it could not possibly have eradicated the problems of poverty and economic depression that English society experienced in the 1590s, they feel that it may have helped to maintain stability in one important respect. Their somewhat speculative view is that in many cases matters would have been worse without the legislation. Attempting to explain why the hardships of the 1590s did not lead to widespread disorder, Barry Coward (18) draws attention to 'a system of poor relief that may have mitigated the worst effects of poverty. It may also have helped to tighten the bonds of patronage between rich and poor and therefore to keep the poor well away from the brink of rebellion.' It helped to convince the 'victims' of economic depression that the government was on their side and, if we accept the argument that the government's main aim was to maintain order, this was no mean achievement.

A consensus now seems to have emerged as to the effectiveness of social and economic legislation in the late sixteenth century. It is accepted that such legislation was a joint effort, and increasingly accepted that it was an impressive one. 'Taken together,' Barry Coward concludes, 'private charity, municipal schemes, government orders and parliamentary statutes are a remarkable response to the early modern poverty problem.' If this combined operation could not significantly reduce the problems of poverty at the time it is possible that its real impact was felt later, in the early seventeenth century, as attitudes slowly changed and resistance slowly broke down. 'The campaign against vagrants and beggars and against indiscriminate alms-giving grew in vigour,' Paul Slack concludes. 'By 1603 some of the old ideals were in retreat.' Above all, the study of this late Tudor legislation illustrates a great truth about Tudor government as a whole. Ultimately, its success depended upon a community of interest between central and local authorities. If government policy was broadly successful in preserving order and stability in the localities, it was less because it successfully treated the problems of poverty and dearth than because it represented interests and attitudes that were shared by local governors. The effectiveness of such legislation, Peter Ramsey reminds us, 'depended upon the good pleasure of the country gentry, and they enforced only those parts of it that accorded with their interests and prejudices. They might cooperate to keep down wages, but not to pull down enclosures.'

Questions

1. Were local social and economic problems more effectively addressed at the end of Elizabeth's reign than at the beginning?

2. For what reasons was the government concerned with local social and economic problems in the second half of the sixteenth century?

SOURCES

1. HENRY VII AND THE EARL OF KILDARE

Source A: part of the instructions given to John Estrete, who travelled to Ireland in 1486 to persuade the Earl of Kildare to travel to England to confirm his allegiance to Henry VII.

Item, his Grace [i.e. Henry] trusteth that upon mutual sight and communication had betwixt his Grace and his said cousin [i.e. Kildare], his Grace shall the rather be inclined to take his said cousin into his high favour and grace, and his said cousin on his part shall much the better be encouraged, moved stirred truly and fastly to serve his Grace.

Item, the said John Estrete shall say that upon the said earl's coming and being with the King, the King shall benignly, tenderly and largely take him into the favour of his Grace as ever did King Edward IV, and in so ample wise depart with him as shall be to the increase of his honour, profit and preferring, and at the same time enlarge his grant of his said office of Deputy Lieutenant for ix or x years to his desire.

Source B: entries in the *Calendar of Carew* for 1487. These are entitled 'Lambert, a boy, an organ maker's son, crowned in the city of Dublin as King of England'.

The Earl of Kildare, then Governor of this realm of Ireland, with the assistance of the Lords Spiritual and Temporal, and Commons, of the north part of Ireland, in the castle of Dublin, crowned the aforesaid boy as King of England and Lord of Ireland, and so proclaimed him; the said Earl and nobility and citizens of Dublin following him as their king, unto whom all the north of Ireland was obedient as their king and lord.

Source C: part of a letter from the 'Lords of Ireland' to Henry VII, concerning Henry's request that Kildare should travel to London to consult with him in person, 1492.

Our right good lord, Gerald, Earl of Kildare, your Deputy Lieutenant in this your land of Ireland hath showed unto us your gracious letters whereby we have well understood your gracious mind in the same that you would have our said good lord to your noble presence, to the intent that he might know thereby your noble mind. Gracious Lord, we understand that he is bounden and sworn to be your true and faithful subject and liegeman as straitly [strictly] and as sure as ever was any subject to his prince: the which oath and assurance our good lord hath well and truly kept to this time. And, gracious lord, forasmuch as we understand the great dangers and eminent perils that should fall if he should depart out of this your land as well by your Irish enemies as otherwise; for when our good lord was sick, divers of the mightiest of your Irish enemies conferred together and noised a division between them of your lands in these parts. And in his said sickness there were divers of your subjects robbed, spoiled and taken prisoners and many other great hurts done. And by the oaths that we have done to your Highness that is true without feigning.

Source D: part of a letter from the Earl of Kildare to the Earl of Ormond, in which Kildare complains of Henry's suspicion towards him, 11 February 1493.

I am accused to the King, as I understand, that I should have lain [i.e. that I am said to have lain] with the French lad that was supported with [by] your cousin and mine, the Earl of Desmond, and that I should aid, support, and comfort him with goods and messages. Whereas I never lay with him, nor aided, comforted, nor supported him with goods nor in any other manner wise, as the lords of this land have certified his Highness at this time. Whereunto I pray you give credence, and to be my good cousin at this time, whereby I may the sooner attain my petitions to the King's grace. This land was never destroyed till now, what by reason of the coming down of your base cousin with the King's Irish enemies to set his most noble authority in danger.

Source E: an extract from *The Book of Howth*. It deals with the Earl of Kildare's summons to London in August 1496 to answer charges relating to his conduct in Ireland and, in particular, to disputes between himself and the Bishop of Meath.

After the Earl had his pardon, and came to Dublin, and so sent to England, and brought to the King, to answer such things that was laid to his charge. Amongst all other, the Bishop of Meath being there, did charge the Earl with sundry matters of great importance, of which matters the Earl could not make answer, but stayed his tongue awhile; for he said that the Bishop was learned, and so was not he, and those matters was long agone out of his mind, though he had done them, and so forgotten.

The King answered, and bade him choose a counsellor whom he would have in England. 'Shall I choose now?' said the Earl. 'Well, I see no better man than you, and by Saint Bride, I will choose none other.' The King laughed and made sport, and said, 'A wiser man might have chosen worse.' 'Well,' said the Bishop, 'he is as you see, for all Ireland cannot rule yonder gentleman.' 'No?' said the King, 'Then he is meet [suited] to rule all Ireland, seeing all Ireland cannot rule him'; and so made the Earl Deputy of Ireland during his life, and so sent him to his country with great gifts, and so the Earl came to Ireland.

Source F: an extract from the Irish chronicle, *Annals of the Four Masters*, describing a campaign against Irish chieftains in Clanrickard and Galway, in 1504.

A great army was mustered by the Lord Justice, Gerald, the son of Thomas, Earl of Kildare. He was joined first by the chieftains of Leath-Chuinn, then by the principal chieftains of Kinel-Connell. There came also to the same muster the chiefs of Ulster, except O'Neill. These numerous forces marched, without stopping, till they arrived in Clanrickard. MacWilliam of Clanrickard mustered a great army to give them battle. A fierce battle was fought between them, such as had not been known of in latter times. The battle was at length gained against MacWilliam, O'Brien and the chiefs of Leath-Mhogha; and a great slaughter was made of them; and of the nine battalions which were in solid battle array, there survived only one broken battalion. A countless number of the Lord Justice's forces were also slain, though they routed the others before them, and on the following day the Lord Justice proceeded to Galway, carrying with him, as prisoners, the two sons, and also a daughter of MacWilliam.

Questions

1. Explain the following references that occur in these sources: 'take him into the favour of his Grace as ever did King Edward IV' (Source A); 'your Irish enemies' (Source C); 'the French lad' (source D).
2. What impression is gained from Sources C and F about Kildare's status within Ireland?
3. To what extent do Sources C and D provide convincing proof of Kildare's loyalty to Henry at the height of the Warbeck conspiracy?
*4. 'The aims of Henry VII and of the Earl of Kildare changed very little in the twenty years after 1485; they simply learned to cooperate with one another.' How far is this view supported by these documents?

Worked answer

*4. [The question requires the student to deploy the information gained from the sources, much of which will have been used to answer the previous questions, in order to form a judgement on the problem posed here. Although it may be tempting to work through source by source, a more fluent and coherent answer will be achieved by dividing the problem into distinct issues. What were Henry's aims at either end of this time scale? What were Kildare's? The final problem, whether the two truly learned to cooperate with each other, can then be dealt with as a separate issue. The student should also be aware that the answer may depend, not just upon the content of each source, but upon its reliability. An answer that provides some assessment of reliability is likely to score more highly than one that takes the contents of the sources entirely at face value.]

Source A indicates the relationship that Henry VII hoped to have with Kildare in the first year of his reign. He proposes an orthodox, feudal relationship in which he will be Kildare's 'good lord' and will maintain Kildare in office, as long as the Earl serves him faithfully. Ten years later, as Source E illustrates, he did indeed place Kildare in a very similar position, confirming his offices and honours in Ireland after the Earl had been brought to London to submit to Henry and to answer charges about his conduct. It might be claimed that neither source is completely reliable. Given the weakness of his political position in 1486, Henry might have had good reason to win over Kildare with promises that he did not intend to keep. The conversation in Source E, on the other hand, is anecdotal and is not corroborated by other sources. Nevertheless, both documents do reflect the solution that Henry adopted, and which was probably the only solution available to him.

Kildare's own behaviour is less consistent. Source B, from an Irish chronicle with no obvious bias against Kildare, clearly shows his support for the pretender Lambert Simnel. Indeed, this source is consistent with what we know of Kildare's actions in 1487. Five or six years later (Sources C and D), Kildare's behaviour is much more ambiguous. Both he (Source D) and his supporters (Source C) protest his loyalty to Henry, claiming that he had not acted in support of Perkin Warbeck, and that he had protected the King's interests against his 'Irish enemies'. Although one can easily find reasons why the Irish nobility might have lied to protect the greatest of their number, Kildare was less likely to lie to a kinsman who knew the truth of the matter in any case. Both sources suggest that Kildare was now eager to convince Henry of his loyalty, but that the King was not so easily persuaded. Source F shows Kildare exercising his office in 1504 by crushing the opposition of some of the chieftains of western Ireland. Although it is quite possible that such action served Kildare's own interests, there is no doubt that these campaigns also served the interests of English government in Ireland.

In conclusion, several of the sources suggest that Kildare was slow to trust or to cooperate with Henry. Although required to come to England in 1486 (Source A), he did not do so until 1496 (Source E), and then under duress. The sources suggest three possible reasons for this: outright disloyalty on Kildare's part (Source B), fear of what would happen in his absence (Source C), or fear on Kildare's part that he would be 'framed' by his enemies (Source D). Overall, the sources suggest that, although Henry VII was relatively consistent in the role that he planned for Kildare, the Earl took some time to appreciate that his best course of action was to cooperate with the English crown.

SOURCES

2. THE ELIZABETHAN POOR LAWS

Source G: from an Act for the Relief of the Poor, 1563, the first Elizabethan Poor Law.

To the intent that idle and loitering persons and valiant beggars may be avoided, and the impotent, feeble and lame, which are the poor in very deed, should be hereafter relieved and well provided for: be it enacted . . .

That yearly upon the Sunday next after Midsummer day, in every city, borough and town corporate, the mayor, bailiffs and other head officers, and in every other parish of the country the parson, vicar or curate and churchwardens shall have written in a register as well the names of the inhabitants and householders within their city or parish, as also the names of all such impotent, aged and needy persons, which are not able to live of themselves nor with their own labour. And [the various officers named above] shall appoint yearly two able persons or more, to be gatherers or collectors of the charitable alms of all the residue of the people inhabiting in the parish.

Source H: from an Act for the Punishment of Vagabonds and for the Relief of the Poor and Impotent, 1572, the second Elizabethan Poor Law.

Where all the parts of the realm of England and Wales be presently with rogues, vagabonds and sturdy beggars exceedingly pestered, by means whereof daily happeneth in the same realm horrible murders, thefts and other outrages, be it enacted . . .

That all persons above the age of fourteen years, being rogues, vagabonds or sturdy beggars, shall upon their apprehension be brought before one of the justices of the peace or mayor or chief officer of cities, boroughs and towns corporate; and if such persons be duly convict of his or her roguish or vagabond trade of life, that then immediately he or she shall be grievously whipped and burnt through the grissle of the right ear with a hot iron of the compass of an inch about.

And forasmuch as charity would that poor, aged and impotent persons should as necessarily be provided for, it is enacted that the justices of the peace, mayors, sheriffs, bailiffs and other officers make diligent search and inquiry of all aged, poor, impotent and decayed persons; and shall also number [count] all the said poor people; and that done, they shall assess all the inhabitants dwelling within the said limits [of the parish or town] to such weekly charge as they and every one of them shall weekly contribute to the relief of the said poor people. And if any person being able to further this charitable work will obstinately refuse to give towards the relief of the said poor people, the said obstinate person shall be brought before two justices of the peace and abide such order therein as the said justices shall appoint.

Source I: from an Act for the Setting of the Poor on Work, 1576, the third Elizabethan Poor Law.

Be it ordained that in every city or town corporate within this realm a competent store and stock of wool, hemp flax, iron or other stuff by order of the mayor shall be provided. The said stores or stocks to be committed to the custody of such persons as shall by the mayor or other head officers be appointed. Which persons shall henceforth be called the collectors and governors of the poor, to the intent that every such poor and needy person able to do any work shall not for want of work go abroad either begging or committing pilferings or other misdemeanours.

And if hereafter any such person able to do any such work shall refuse to work, or taking such work shall spoil or embezzle the same, he, she or they shall be received into a house of correction, there to be straightly [strictly] kept, as well in diet as in work, and also punished from time to time.

Source J: from an Act for the Relief of the Poor, the Poor Law of 1601.

Be it enacted by the authority of this present Parliament, that the churchwardens of every parish, and four, three, or two substantial householders to be nominated yearly, shall be called overseers of the poor of the same parish: and they or the greater part of them shall take order from time to time, with the consent of two or more justices of the peace, for setting to work of the children whose parents shall not be thought able to keep and maintain their children; and also for setting to work all such persons married or unmarried who have no means to maintain them, or use no ordinary or daily trade of life to get their living by.

And be it further enacted that it shall be lawful for the said churchwardens and overseers, or the greater part of them, by the assent of two justices of the peace aforesaid, to bind any such children to be apprentices, where they shall see convenient, till such man-child shall come to the age of four and twenty years, and such woman-child to the age of one and twenty years, or the time of her marriage.

Source K: part of a census on poor relief conducted in Sheffield, January 1615.

It appeareth that there are in the town of Sheffield 2207 people; of which there are 725 which are not able to live without the charity of their neighbours. These all begging poor. 100 householders which relieve others. These are but poor artificers; among them there is not one which can keep a team [of oxen] on his own land. 160 householders not able to relieve others.

Questions

1. Define the following terms that appear in the sources: 'valiant beggars' (Source G); 'house of correction' (Source I); 'house-holders which relieve others' (Source K).
*2. What different categories of poor persons are identified in Sources G, H and I? What different methods do these acts use to deal with them?
3. On the strength of these sources, summarise the main agencies available to the Elizabethan state for the implementation of social policy in the localities.
4. 'In England in the second half of the sixteenth century, poverty was a crime to be punished, rather than a social problem to be cured.' How far do these sources, and any other evidence known to you, support this statement?

Worked answer

*2. [The question is essentially an exercise in comprehension. It tests the student's ability to understand the language in which the legislation was couched, and to detect through it the distinctions drawn between 'sturdy' and 'impotent' poor, as well as the different strategies employed either to punish or relieve them. The student can only afford a limited amount of time on a largely factual question of this kind, and must provide a concise overview of the sources, avoiding temptation largely to paraphrase them in more contemporary language.]

The sources are all extracts from the Poor Laws passed in Parliament between 1563 and 1576. Sources G and H distinguish two different kinds of pauper. The first of these are those 'idle and loitering persons' who live by begging and theft, and who make no attempt to find work. These are clearly distinguished from 'the impotent, feeble and lame' who are physically unable to work. The third Poor Law (Source I) also sets out to deal with a third category of poor, those who are willing to work, but who can find no employment. These are dealt with in the 1576 act by being provided with raw materials by the local authorities and set to work, so that they do not have to resort to begging. Sources H and I make it clear that paupers in the first category are to be treated as criminals. The 1572 act (Source H) subjected them to corporal punishment, while the third Poor Law (Source I) provided for the establishment of 'houses of correction' to deal with those who refused the work provided. Sources G and H both recognise that the 'impotent poor' must be given financial relief, but they provide that relief in different ways. While the 1563 act relied upon voluntary contributions of 'charitable alms', the act of 1572 imposes the collection of a compulsory, assessed poor rate, and provides for those who refuse to pay to be brought before the JPs and duly punished.

6

THE ROLE OF PARLIAMENT

BACKGROUND NARRATIVE

The English Parliament developed from the 'Grand Councils' occasionally summoned by the crown from the mid-thirteenth century. Their dual purpose was to provide the monarch with advice from the political nation on specific issues and to act as a superior court of justice. The format that the Tudors inherited, and the assumptions governing the membership and functions of the assembly, had existed for a little over a century. The aristocracy of the realm sat by right in the House of Lords, and were divided into two categories. The nobility, who gained their titles either by birth or by service to the crown, constituted the Lords Temporal, while the leading churchmen constituted the Lords Spiritual. The lower chamber, the House of Commons, was also divided into two categories. The Knights of the Shires, two representatives from each of the English counties, enjoyed greater status at the start of the century, but this was steadily eroded by the Burgesses, the representatives of enfranchised urban boroughs, whose numbers increased steadily in the course of the sixteenth century.

For a century before the first Tudor Parliament met, the institution had played two major roles in the government of the realm. Its legislative acts constituted the most authoritative form of law. Such measures acquired the status of statute law, recognised as binding in the courts of the realm, and it was thus a matter of great importance that the will of the governors should be enshrined in these acts of Parliament. It had been established since the mid-fifteenth century that, for bills to become law, they required the consent of King, Lords and Commons alike. The second function was the voting of taxes which also, therefore, had the force of law. Such financial grants were indispensable to the crown, especially in times of war or of other emergency, when the monarch's income from his own landed and feudal sources was inadequate. As the sixteenth century progressed this taxation more frequently took the form of a subsidy, a fixed sum based upon the value of goods or of land, rather than upon the more old-fashioned 'tenths' or 'fifteenths', taxes based upon an estimated proportion of a tax-payer's landed wealth.

Although historians have often concentrated predominantly upon the role of Parliament in national government, it also played an extremely important role in the functioning of local politics and patronage. Having granted the crown the taxes and the laws that it required, as it usually did, Parliament would then expect to spend some time on private bills. These were usually matters of local importance, put forward by local representatives who thus advanced their own interests, and also those of local people who turned to them for patronage and favours.

For all its undoubted importance, Parliament, throughout the sixteenth century, had little or no independent power base, beyond the will of the monarch and of the government. Summoned by royal writ, it was also dissolved (brought to an end) or prorogued (adjourned to a later date) entirely at the will of the monarch. During its sittings, furthermore, the business of the Commons would be directed by the Speaker, invariably nominated by the crown, and observed and influenced by royal ministers sitting in both houses.

ANALYSIS (1): WHAT ROLE DID PARLIAMENT PLAY DURING THE REIGNS OF THE FIRST TWO TUDORS?

The most authoritative of recent writers on Henry VII, Professor Chrimes, spends little time on the parliamentary history of the reign. 'Little or nothing of much significance occurred in the history of Parliament in the reign of Henry VII,' he wrote. 'There were no significant innovations in procedure; no change in composition or electoral arrangements; few legislative measures enacted were of any great importance.' (1) Such a judgement must be assessed in the context of the debate that has taken place in the course of the last four decades about the development of Parliament, and which is outlined in greater detail in the second analysis in this chapter. Chrimes's conclusions are undoubtedly correct if one judges in terms of the growth of parliamentary independence, and if one looks for the development in this period of an institution aiming to restrict, or capable of challenging the authority of, the monarch. M.A.R. Graves speaks for a generation of revisionist historians, however, when he writes that Parliament 'deserves to be studied in terms of its importance within the sixteenth century, not merely with an eye to future conflict'. (2) In that context our priority must be to assess the precise role played by Parliament within the government of Henry VII and Henry VIII.

Two central facts stand out in this period about the constitutional role of the English Parliament. One is that the King was under no obligation to summon the body. Thus, Henry VII met Parliament only twice in the last fourteen years of his reign, while his son summoned only one in the fourteen years between 1515 and 1529. At other times, however, it is equally clear that Parliament provided the crown with facilities which, under certain circumstances, were essential. Five Parliaments were summoned in the years between 1485 and 1495, as Henry VII established his regime and resisted pretenders to his throne. Parliamentary grants of taxation constituted an indispensable source of income for the crown, particularly in time of war. Henry VII gained a total estimated by G.W. Bernard (3) at 312,000 pounds in the form of a life grant of tunnage and poundage (1485), fifteenths and tenths (1487, 1489, 1491, 1497), a poll tax on merchants trading into England (1487), taxes based upon the income of the laity (1489, 1497, 1504), and two feudal aids (1504). Wolsey, too, despite his difficulties in 1523, gained grants in each of the six parliamentary sessions between 1510 and 1515, amounting to some 287,000 pounds. The second essential role played by Parliament lay in its legal function of enacting and establishing statute law. Statute law served the first two Tudors in several respects. In both reigns, the first parliamentary session was of great importance. For Henry VII it acknowledged his claim to the throne, attainted his enemies, and reversed attainders against himself and his supporters. While his son's needs were less pressing, his first Parliament still provided an important opportunity for a public relations exercise, in which the attainders against Empson and Dudley, the most unpopular of his father's ministers, were central. This appears to confirm the conclusion of M.A.R. Graves that during this period 'parliaments were called to service royal government', for

Parliament met most frequently when the King had greatest need of it. Henry VII had little need of it in the last decade of his life and there is some justification for David Loades's comment that 'in 1509 an observer could well have been forgiven for thinking that if the monarchy continued to be strong, Parliament would gradually become an irrelevance'. (4) It is equally true that Henry VII's Parliaments were considerably less exciting and less radical than many that had met during the Wars of the Roses. Graves comments that 'they met less frequently, deposed no monarch, and impeached no minister or favourite. They granted tunnage and poundage for life [and] established no principle of "redress before supply".'

Two political factors, however, ensured the survival and development of Parliament. One was Henry VIII's decision to exhaust his financial resources on wars with France, with its automatic imperative for extra taxation. Indeed, it seems possible that Henry consciously chose parliamentary taxation as an alternative to the unpopular, extortionate methods employed by the crown in the last years of his father's reign. The other was the great crisis of the King's divorce in the late 1520s and early 1530s. Then, for the first time under Henry VIII, it was the legal, rather than the financial, functions of Parliament that recommended the institution to a government badly in need of all the allies it could find.

This is not to say that Parliament before 1529 served as a 'rubber stamp', tamely passing whatever legislation the government put before it. There is ample evidence of contention in these early Tudor Parliaments, from 1485 when the attainder bill demanded by Henry VII against his defeated enemies 'sore was questioned with', through the Commons' resistance to the subsidy demands in 1504, to the famous session of 1523. This proved to be the most difficult early Tudor Parliament to manage. Wolsey's requests for unusually high levels of taxation were strongly resisted in the Commons although, in the end, he succeeded in wringing significant sums from it. Historians in recent years have interpreted this opposition in two ways, neither of which suggests any great degree of institutional independence on the part of the Commons. Most frequently the protests have been seen as an indication that contemporary MPs were extremely sensitive to measures that threatened the landed and financial interests of their class. More recently, however, M.A.R. Graves has speculated that the difficulties of 1523 in particular may have arisen from the attempts of Wolsey's political enemies, men such as Norfolk, Suffolk and Northumberland, to forward their factional opposition to the minister by mobilising their clients in the House of Commons. Such an interpretation would confirm the contemporary perception of Parliament as an extension of the usual channels of royal, courtly and conciliar government.

There is general agreement, however, about the importance of the Parliament that sat between 1529 and 1536, the Reformation Parliament. In his definitive account, S.E. Lehmberg (5) was not prepared to see this Parliament essentially as 'servicing royal government'. In Lehmberg's interpretation many members entered the Parliament in 1529 with a distinct, anti-clerical agenda of their own, so that the legislation of that period represented a genuinely cooperative venture between the King and his lay subjects gathered in Parliament. For many subsequent commentators, however, the longevity of the Reformation Parliament indicates that, while the government clearly understood that Parliament could serve as a valuable ally in the political and legal struggle with the Church, it was uncertain how best to utilise it. First Parliament helped the King to exert pressure upon the English Church. Then, more radically, its law-making functions were exploited to provide the legal basis for the break from Rome, and the establishment of an independent English Church under the authority of the King. Whether as a joint venture, or as a massive governmental exercise in power politics, there can be no doubt that by the end of Henry's reign Parliament had broken new ground in many respects. In 1533 and 1534 the Reformation Parliament legislated away the Pope's legal authority over the English Church and declared Henry to be 'Supreme Head on Earth of the Church of England'. It gave legal form to the clergy's surrender of their separate status and it legislated on the future succession to the throne. On the strength of such precedents, statute law legislated in the remainder of Henry's reign on an unprecedented range of matters. These included the suppression of semi-independent political 'franchises' (1536), the transfer of monastic property to the crown (1536 and 1539), details of 'correct' religious doctrine (1539) and the reform of local government in Wales (1543). The authority of statute law as a sanction against the enemies of the crown was such in these years that the Countess of Salisbury (1539), Thomas Cromwell (1540) and the Duke of Norfolk (1547) were all condemned for treason without any other form of trial. In the process the events of the 1530s also transformed the House of Lords by destroying the balance there between the Lords Temporal and the Lords Spiritual. The removal of twenty-nine abbots upon the dissolution of their abbeys, even when offset by the creation of several new bishoprics, left the Lords as a substantially temporal body, largely in tune with the priorities of the Court and of the political nation.

Statute law was now capable of resolving a wider range of issues than ever before, and this extension of the competence of Parliament had taken place entirely in cooperation with the crown and entirely in the royal interest. By the death of Henry VIII, the history of the English Parliament had moved in a very different direction from that of its continental equivalents, such as the Estates General in France and the Cortes in Castile. While those institutions degenerated and played little constructive role in the policies of those states, Parliament became practically omnicompetent and an essential element in the government of the realm. So far from developing initiatives and agendas of its own, however, Parliament developed this enhanced status because, closely managed and directed by the King and his ministers, it proved an invaluable ally in the implementation of royal policy. While no one doubted that the King was the highest force in the land, and by far the strongest element in the parliamentary partnership, the concept of 'the King in Parliament' had taken on a widely recognised meaning. The monarch was regarded as being at his most powerful when he acted in concert with the greatest interest groups in his realm.

Questions

1. For what purposes did the crown summon Parliament in the years between 1485 and 1529?
2. To what extent would you agree with the judgement that 'for the first fifty years of the Tudor era, Parliament was entirely subservient to the crown'?

ANALYSIS (2): DID THE ROLE AND IMPORTANCE OF PARLIAMENT WITHIN THE GOVERNMENTAL SYSTEM CHANGE SIGNIFICANTLY DURING THE REIGN OF ELIZABETH?

For two decades after the Second World War the historiography of Elizabethan parliaments was dominated by the work of Sir John Neale. (6) Neale developed the conclusions of the American scholar, Wallace Notestein, (7) that in the reign of Elizabeth the House of Commons began to emerge as the senior partner in the parliamentary relationship with the crown and the House of Lords. Furthermore, this period witnessed the growth of those habits of independence and political opposition to the crown that were to culminate in the civil conflict of the next century. At the beginning of Elizabeth's reign, in Neale's interpretation, a vociferous Protestant minority in the Commons, the puritan 'choir', played a crucial role in the shaping of a religious settlement significantly more radical than Elizabeth would ideally have desired. Such men persisted in their attempts further to radicalise the English Church, and to exclude the Catholic Mary Stuart from the succession. At the same time radical MPs sought to preserve and to strengthen the privileges of the Lower House, resisting royal efforts to circumvent them.

Revision of this interpretation began in earnest in the early 1980s, and was particularly influenced by the work of Norman Jones, (8) G.R. Elton (9) and M.A.R. Graves. (10) Professor Jones undermined Neale's case by disproving the existence of any coordinated puritan opposition group within Elizabeth's early Parliaments. From that basis, Professor Elton reinterpreted the pressure that Elizabeth encountered either to marry or to establish an order of succession that excluded the Queen of Scots. He now saw such pressure as emanating from loyal members of the Council. Unable to persuade the Queen to their way of thinking in the Council Chamber, they sought to exert pressure in an alternative political forum, in which they might benefit from the wider support of the political nation. Considered in this light, it seems clear that Elizabeth's Parliaments were still summoned 'to service royal government'. In 1559 Parliament had familiar tasks to perform in installing a new monarch and in revising once again the settlement of religion. The sessions of 1571 and 1572 were preoccupied with 'the great cause' of Mary, Queen of Scots, and from the mid-1580s onwards the war with Spain occupied centre stage, with its serious implications for crown finances and national security. Similarly, the crown sought and gained financial subsidies in all but one of the thirteen sessions of the reign.

The tensions between parliamentary privileges and the royal prerogative once stood at the centre of the debate on Elizabethan Parliaments. It was clearly established that, when Parliament was in session, MPs enjoyed such privileges as freedom to speak their minds on the matters put before them, and freedom from arrest. Neale, however, claimed that the reign saw these freedoms increasingly interpreted in the Commons as constitutional rights, rather than temporary privileges granted in the crown's interest. Paul Wentworth's demand to be allowed to continue the debate on the succession, despite the Queen's displeasure (1566), or the protests of his brother Peter at royal management of the House (1576), were seen as crucial stages in the development of parliamentary independence. Divorced from the events of the seventeenth century, however, such incidents now seem relatively insignificant, appearing, in the phrase of Michael Graves, as 'tactless outbursts [by] loners without support'. David Loades is not quite so dismissive of the Wentworths. (11) He accepts that they were unrepresentative of opinion in the Commons, yet feels that they provided 'a genuine expression of the seriousness with which the members [of the Commons] were beginning to take their role in the formation of policy'. In the case of freedom from arrest, similarly, the Commons broadly accepted the crown's priorities. Strickland's Case (1571) and FitzHerbert's Case (1593) confirmed that the immunity of an MP did not apply when the case was brought against him by the crown.

One of the most important elements of revision has concerned the role played in the latter part of the sixteenth century by the House of Lords. Whereas Neale and Notestein saw the proportion of legislation initiated in the Commons as an indication that this House had become the focus of the parliamentary process, it now seems unwise to see any linear progression in this respect. Michael Graves emphasises that the focus shifted from one chamber to the other according to the location from which the great ministers of the crown exerted their managerial influence: 'It remains possible', he concludes, 'that in the early Elizabethan parliaments the Commons was the operative centre, though not for the reasons argued by Neale. Sir William Cecil sat there.' Thus, when Cecil was elevated to the peerage in 1572 as Lord Burghley, it was the Lords that became the centre of the government's management of Parliament. With the decline and eventual death of Burghley (1598), influence passed to Sir Robert Cecil, his son and heir to his patronage and authority, sitting in the Commons. It also seems unwise to consider the two Houses too distinctly as separate entities. Such was the degree of patronage exercised by some of the greatest territorial magnates, men such as Bedford, Leicester and Shrewsbury, that a significant number of MPs in the Commons would have been their clients, therefore pursuing similar political and legislative agendas.

Above all, recent writers have stressed how few resources Parliament possessed with which to oppose the government. 'In this reign', concluded Professor Elton, 'neither Lords nor Commons constituted any sort of threat to the crown. We have heard so much about the rising power of the Lower House . . . that it comes as something of a surprise to discover how little power the Commons especially possessed.' It remained the case that Parliament only sat when the Queen wanted or needed it to do so, and it was only in session for 140 weeks in a reign of forty-five years. Once the Commons was elected and in session, the government exercised considerable control over the agenda and the conduct of debate. The Speaker, for instance, was invariably a crown nominee. Elizabeth's reign must be regarded as the high point in the governmental art of managing Tudor Parliaments, but not in the manner that Neale perceived, talented and cynical ministers using Machiavellian tactics to restrain and thwart a hostile House. The supreme parliamentary manager of the century, William Cecil, did not only work to ensure the safe conduct of royal business. He often also undertook the reverse process, marshalling and focusing parliamentary pressure upon the Queen in such essentially loyal causes as the royal marriage, the succession, and the fate of Mary Stuart. When the risk of offending the Queen became too great, the councillors made use of their 'men of business' within the House. These were MPs without public office, clients of individual councillors, who promoted delicate measures which the councillors considered to be in the interests of the realm. The most notable of these, Thomas Norton (MP from 1558 to 1581), was active in the parliamentary campaigns concerning the Queen's marriage, the succession and the further reform of the Church. Such councillors, then, may not always have worked strictly in accordance with the Queen's wishes, but it is clear that they perceived themselves always as managing the Commons in the Queen's interests.

Yet significant developments did occur in Elizabeth's reign. In particular, the latter part of the century witnessed the continuing triumph of statute law as an indispensable institution within English political and social life. What had been an increasingly important tool of government in the first half of the century 'now came home to roost', in the words of Michael Graves, 'in the relative stability of Elizabeth's long reign. Parliaments became the occasions for the statutory resolution and satisfaction of all manner of local, personal, economic and legal problems and grievances.' Indeed, in his later work Professor Elton considered that it was unwise to concentrate upon the national business conducted in Parliament, for such matters were 'no more than an occasional intrusion' upon the more parochial concerns that pre-occupied most MPs. In addition, some elements of Neale's argument must be retained as important aspects of constitutional development, although not necessarily as harbingers of the seventeenth-century conflicts. The membership of the House of Commons certainly increased considerably, from 402 in 1559, to 440 in 1572 and 460 in 1584. There is little dispute either about the role played in this increase by the desire of major political figures to extend their own influence by expanding the parliamentary representation of areas in which they exercised patronage. David Loades is eager to retain two other important elements of Neale's argument. He emphasises the extent to which the Commons gained a degree of control over its own affairs, establishing, for instance, by 1593 a legal right to adjudicate in electoral disputes. He also confirms how the length and frequency of parliamentary sessions allowed the emergence of the 'Parliament man', a more experienced breed of representative, sitting in several successive Parliaments, and therefore gaining greater expertise in the tactics, precedents and procedure of the House. Recent research also confirms Neale's conclusions that members of the county gentry came increasingly to represent urban boroughs in the Commons.

As in the case of earlier Tudor assemblies, however, this broad community of interest cannot obscure genuine instances of tension between the Queen and her Parliaments. Elizabeth's first Parliament provided an example unparalleled in the sixteenth century, of active opposition to the wishes of the crown when three bills on religion were firmly rejected by the House of Lords in February 1559. With the issues of the royal Supremacy, uniformity and the repeal of the Marian anti-heresy laws suspended in limbo, it took an unusual combination of management and direct political 'muscle' to force through a religious settlement acceptable to the new Queen. A further major confrontation occurred in the last two Parliaments of the reign, in 1597 and 1601, over the crown's practice of granting trading monopolies to favoured courtiers and their clients in return for large sums of ready cash. For John Guy, (12) the monopolies dispute was 'the ugliest in Parliament during the Tudor period', but it is now primarily interpreted, like the confrontations of Henry VII's and Henry VIII's reigns, as an expression of concern at damage done to the financial interests of many MPs.

It may not be coincidental that such issues arose in the final years of the reign when the deaths of Burghley, Walsingham, Hatton, Knollys and others had brought the 'golden age' of parliamentary management to an end. This is one reason, perhaps, for anticipating changes in parliamentary relationships in the first decades of the seventeenth century. The role of Parliament had developed subtly and significantly under Elizabeth, although not in such a way as to justify Neale's conclusion that the reign saw the development of 'the art of opposition, which might be considered the outstanding contribution of the period to parliamentary history'. Jennifer Loach (13) replaces this judgement with the conclusion that 'the century after 1530 was one of substantial harmony in the relationship between crown and Parliament, and that the institution itself served the needs of both ruler and ruled satisfactorily until at least the 1620s.'

Questions

1. How valid is the argument that Parliament achieved a significant degree of political independence from the crown during the reign of Elizabeth?
2. 'The governmental priorities of the Elizabethan House of Commons were essentially the same as those of the Queen herself.' Do you agree?

SOURCES

This group of sources is concerned with the competence and authority of parliamentary statute, and the ways in which this authority was perceived at various points in the sixteenth century.

1. THE AUTHORITY OF PARLIAMENTARY STATUTE

Source A: from Christopher St German, *A Dialogue Betwixt a Doctor of Divinity and a Student in the Laws of England*, 1530.

The law of man, the which sometimes is called the law positive, is derived by reason as a thing which is necessarily following the law of reason and the law of God. In every law positive well made is somewhat of the law of reason and of the law of God.

Every man's law must be consonant to the law of God. And therefore the law of princes, nor the commandments of prelates, the statutes of communities, nor yet the ordinance of the Church is not right wise nor obligatory but [unless] it be consonant to the law of God.

The sixth ground of the law of England standeth in divers statutes made by our sovereign lord the King and his progenitors [predecessors], and by the Lords spiritual and temporal and the Commons of the whole realm in divers Parliaments, in such cases where the law of reason, the law of God, customs, maxims nor other grounds of the law seemed not to be sufficient to punish evil men and to reward good men.

Source B: Sir Thomas More speaking at his trial in 1534, as reported by William Roper in his *Life of Sir Thomas More*.

'Forasmuch as, my lord,' quoth he, 'this indictment is grounded upon an act of Parliament directly repugnant to the laws of God and His Holy Church, the supreme government of which may no temporal prince presume by any law to take upon him, as rightfully belonging to the See of Rome, a spiritual preeminence by the mouth of Our Saviour himself, personally present upon the earth, only to St Peter and his successors, by special prerogative granted. It is therefore in law, amongst Christian men, insufficient to charge any Christian man. You have no authority without the consent of Christians all over the world to make laws against the union of Christendom and you sin gravely in doing so.'

Source C: the Pilgrimage of Grace.

From the interrogation of Robert Aske in the aftermath of the Pilgrimage of Grace, 1536.

Concerning the act to allow the king to bequeath the crown by will, the said Aske saith that he disliked it for several reasons. One was that before the statute no king settled the succession by will, nor was such a law known in this realm. Also if the crown should pass by testament, there would be a great risk of war if it were taken from the heir apparent. It should be settled so that the certainty might appear who should be heir apparent, or else it should be as it were before, the same to go to the very next blood of the King.

Part of Henry VIII's answer to the demands put forward by the rebels involved in the Pilgrimage of Grace, November 1536.

Concerning choosing the Councillors, I have never read, heard nor known that the prince's councillors and prelates should be appointed by rude and ignorant people. As to the suppression of religious houses and monasteries, this is granted by Act of Parliament and not set forth by any councillors upon their mere will.

Source D: part of a letter from Simon Renard to Charles V in which the ambassador recounts a conversation with Lord Paget on the subject of the succession in the event of Queen Mary's death without offspring, 28 November 1553.

The rival claimants would be the Queen of Scotland, who had a real right by descent; the Lady Frances, wife of the Duke of Suffolk, who would also have a claim if the Queen of Scotland were excluded as having been born abroad, as being a Scotswoman and married to the Dauphin of France; and my Lady Elizabeth, who claimed the crown because of the disposition of the late King Henry, authorised by an act of Parliament that had never been repealed. As for the Lady Elizabeth, the Queen would scruple to allow her to succeed because of her heretical opinions [and] illegitimacy. It seemed to [Paget] that, as Parliament had accepted the Lady Elizabeth as proper to succeed, it would be difficult to deprive her of the right she claimed without causing trouble. [Paget] told me that if the Queen desired to induce Parliament to repeal the act regulating the succession, Parliament would, in his opinion, refuse, so the Queen would struggle in vain to have another heir appointed.

Source E: from Sir Thomas Smith, *De Republica Anglorum*, 1565.

The most high and absolute power of the realm of England consisteth in the Parliament. The Parliament abrogateth [abolishes] old laws, maketh new, giveth orders for things past, and for things hereafter to be followed, changeth rights and possessions of private men, legitimateth bastards, establisheth forms of religion, altereth weights and measures, giveth forms of succession to the Crown, defineth of doubtful rights whereof is no law already made, appointeth subsidies, tallies, taxes and impositions, giveth most free pardons and absolutions, restoreth in blood and name as the highest court, condemneth and absolveth them whom the prince will put to the trial. And, to be short, all that ever the people of Rome might do either in *Centuriatis comitiis* or *tributis*, the same may be done by the Parliament of England which representeth and hath the power of the whole realm, both the head and the body. For every Englishman is intended to be there present. And the consent of the Parliament is taken to be every man's consent.

Questions

1. Explain the following references that occur in the sources: 'the act to allow the king to bequeath the crown by will' (Source C); 'because of her heretical opinions [and] illegitimacy' (Source D).
*2. To what extent and on what grounds do Sources A and B disagree with Source E about the authority of parliamentary statute?
3. What evidence is there in these sources to suggest that the competence of statute law was extended between 1530 and 1560?
4. 'The universal authority of statute law had been firmly established and widely accepted by the end of Henry VIII's reign.' How far do these sources, and any other evidence known to you, lead you to accept this judgement?

Worked answer

*2. [The question requires the student to carry out two processes: to detect and summarise similarities and differences in the attitudes of each of these writers towards the authority of parliamentary statute, and briefly to summarise the arguments put forward as justification.]

In Source E, Sir Thomas Smith states that Parliament is the highest authority in the realm, and that the statute law defined by Parliament thus carries comparable influence. The examples that he gives indicate that he considers statute law to be omnicompetent, capable of dealing with any issue that may arise within the realm.

Sources A and B both state, on the other hand, that all human laws are inevitably subordinate to the laws of God, and are invalid unless they rest upon that foundation. Sir Thomas More, in Source B, specifically states that a law which is 'repugnant to the laws of God' should not be obeyed, and clearly identifies two authorities, God and 'the See of Rome', that have an authority superior to that of statute law. St German, in Source A, regards statute law as only one of at least six elements from which English law derives. He clearly does not regard it as the most important.

On a more specific level, Smith claims in Source E that statute law is competent to establish 'forms of religion', precisely the power that Sir Thomas More denies in Source B.

SOURCES

This group of sources investigates the extent and nature of parliamentary privilege, and the counter-arguments of the crown's prerogative.

2. PREROGATIVE AND PRIVILEGE IN ELIZABETH'S PARLIAMENTS

Source F: from the Lord Keeper's speech in reply to the Speaker's petitions for the customary liberties and privileges of the House of Commons, January 1559.

To these petitions the Queen's Majesty hath commanded me to say unto you that her Highness is right well contented to grant them unto you as largely and as liberally as ever they were granted by her noble progenitors [predecessors], with these admonitions and cautions. First, that your access [to the Queen's person] be void of importunity, and for matters needful, and in times convenient. For the third [petition] which is for liberty of speech, wherewith her Highness is right well contented, be so as they be neither unmindful nor uncareful of their duties, reverence and obedience to their sovereign. These admonitions being well remembered, her Majesty thinketh all the said liberties and privileges well granted.

Source G: from the Lord Keeper's speech at the opening of Parliament, 1592.

For liberty of speech her Majesty commandeth me to tell you that to say yea or nay to bills, God forbid that any man should be restrained or afraid to answer according to his best liking, with some short declaration of his reason therein, and therein to have a free voice, which is the very true liberty of the House; not, as some suppose, to speak there of all causes as him listeth [as he pleases], and to frame a form of religion or a state of government as to their idle brains shall seem the meetest [the most fitting]. She sayeth no king fit for his state will suffer such absurdities.

Source H: from Paul Wentworth's *Questions on Privilege*, November 1566.

Whether her Highness's commandment, forbidding the lower house to speak or treat any more of the succession be a breach of the liberty of free speech of the House or not? Whether Mr Controller [Sir Edward Rogers], the Vicechamberlain [Sir Francis Knollys] and Mr Secretary [Sir William Cecil], pronouncing in the House the said commandment in her Highness's name, are of authority sufficient to bind the House in silence on that behalf or not?

Source I: account from the *Journal* of the House of Commons of a speech by Peter Wentworth in the Parliament of 1576.

Amongst other things, Mr Speaker, two things do great hurt in this place: the one is a rumour that runneth about the house and this it is, 'Take heed what you do, the Queen's Majesty liketh not such a matter. Whosoever prefereth it, she will be offended with him.' Or the contrary, 'Her Majesty liketh of such a matter. Whosoever speaketh against it, she will be offended with him.'

The other: sometimes a message is brought into the house, either of commanding or inhibiting, very injurious to the freedom of speech and consultation. I would to God, Mr Speaker, that these two were buried in hell, I mean rumours and messages, for wicked undoubtedly they are.

Upon this speech the house, out of reverent regard for her Majesty's honour, stopped his further proceeding before he had fully finished his speech. Mr Wentworth being sequestered [excluded from] the house it was agreed and ordered that he should be presently committed to the serjeant's ward as prisoner.

Source J: from the *Journal of All the Parliaments during the Reign of Queen Elizabeth*, describing incidents in the Parliament of 1587.

Mr Cope, first using some speeches touching the necessity of a learned ministry offered to the house a bill and book, the bill containing a petition that it might be enacted that all laws now in force touching ecclesiastical government should be void. And that it might be enacted that the book of common prayer now offered and none other might be received into the Church to be used. Whereupon Mr Speaker in effect used this speech: that for her majesty upon this time had commanded the house not to meddle with this matter, he desired that it would please them to spare the reading of it. Notwithstanding the house desired the reading of it. Mr Dalton made a motion against the reading of it, saying that it was not meet [suitable] to be read and thought that this dealing would bring her majesty's indignation against the house thus to enterprise the dealing with those things which her majesty had especially taken into her own charge and discretion.

On Thursday, Mr Cope, Mr Lewknor, Mr Hurleston and Mr Bainbridge were sent for to my Lord Chancellor and by divers of the Privy Council, and from thence to the Tower.

Questions

1. Explain the following references in the sources: 'forbidding the lower house to speak . . . any more of the succession' (Source H): 'the necessity of a learned ministry' (Source J).
2. How consistent is Elizabeth's attitude to the parliamentary privilege of freedom of speech in Sources F and G?
*3. In what ways, according to Sources H and I, did the Wentworth brothers differ from Elizabeth in their interpretation of the privilege of freedom of speech?
4. What evidence is there in these sources of the means available to the crown for the effective control of proceedings in the House of Commons?
5. To what extent do these sources support the claim that the House of Commons sought and achieved a significant degree of political independence in the course of Elizabeth's reign?

Worked answer

*3. [This question tests the student's ability to comprehend and to summarise the content of different sources or sets of sources, and to carry out a comparison between them. The student should be aware that, although the question refers specifically to Sources H and I, it is also necessary to use the information already derived from the previous question about the Queen's conception of parliamentary freedom of speech.]

Sources F and G illustrate Elizabeth's understanding of the concept of freedom of speech within the House of Commons. She perceives the Commons as a conciliar assembly summoned to provide advice on those issues which the crown puts before it, and assumes that it will be constrained by the same considerations of 'reverence and obedience to their sovereign' as apply in all other political activities. More specifically, the Queen clearly forbids the Commons to debate such prerogative matters as the religious settlement and matters pertaining to the status of the monarchy.

The Wentworth brothers, on the other hand, believe that the freedom of speech granted by the crown to the Commons extends to all issues that may be of political or religious concern to the members. In Source H, Paul Wentworth specifically questions the Queen's right to forbid the Commons to 'treat any more of the succession', despite the fact that her commandment is completely consistent with her views expressed in Sources F and G. The succession to the throne obviously falls within the category of 'the state of government' which the Queen considered to be beyond the competence of the Commons. In Source I, his brother Peter objects to the more indirect means used by the government to influence and control debates within the House of Commons, indicating that, in his opinion, freedom of speech is an absolute right and that it should not be restricted in any way.

7

GOVERNMENT OF THE CHURCH

For the first fifty years of the Tudor era the processes of civil government were complicated by the semi-independent status of the Church. The Church constituted a separate entity in two respects. It was governed by a separate hierarchy with a foreign potentate, the Pope, at its head. Within England papal authority was delegated to temporary ambassadors, papal legates, or to the Pope's permanent representatives within the hierarchy of the national Church. England and Wales were divided into two provinces, Canterbury and York, each with its archbishop, although the primacy of Canterbury had been recognised since the eleventh century. The two provinces were subdivided into twenty-two dioceses (rising to twenty-seven by the end of the century), each with a bishop responsible for the conduct of religious life in the component parishes. In addition to this 'secular' clergy, the 'regular' clergy, so called because they lived by a monastic rule (Latin: *regulus*), further complicated the picture.

The Church also maintained a distinct code of law, canon law, which governed spiritual matters throughout Western Europe. As this embraced issues of marriage, divorce, legitimacy and probate of wills, as well as issues of morality, canon law inevitably had a significant impact upon the lives of the laity. In principle the clergy were subject to this law code, rather than to civil law. Such concepts as Benefit of Clergy (whereby criminals might avoid the penalties of civil law if they could prove their clerical status) and Sanctuary (whereby the Church might protect laymen who sought refuge on Church property) were potentially sources of tension between Church and state authorities. Tension might also arise from the respective claims of crown and papacy over the appointment of senior churchmen, and over the taxation of the English Church. To protect its interests the crown could invoke the Statutes of *Praemunire* (1353, 1365 and 1393), which made it illegal to refer cases to foreign courts, and especially to Rome, in matters which came within the competence of the King's courts.

The legislation passed in the 'Reformation Parliament' between 1532 and 1534 had a radical impact upon this dualism. Unable to tolerate or to resolve the obstructions that canon law placed in the way of his divorce and remarriage, Henry VIII used the authority of English statute law to bring about a constitutional revolution. Among much other legislation, the Act in Restraint of Appeals (1533) established that it was illegal to appeal to Rome against a judgement in an English ecclesiastical court, while the Act of Supremacy (1534) transferred to the crown all the powers that previously lay in the hands of the Pope. Between 1536 and 1540 Henry and his ministers used these new powers to destroy the institution of monasticism in England.

With that exception, however, the purpose of the Henrician Reformation was to annex, rather than to destroy, the hierarchy and the legal system of the Church in England. For the rest of the Tudor period, with the exception of Mary's reign, the crown combined control of the organs of state with the control of ecclesiastical law, appointments, revenues, discipline and doctrine within England. If previous monarchs had exercised some of these powers with tacit papal approval, the crown now exercised them all through the authority of statute law. With two exceptions, such powers were exercised through the traditional ecclesiastical channels. One exception occurred in Henry's reign, when he briefly delegated his authority to Thomas Cromwell, as 'Vicegerent in Spirituals' (1535–40), and the other when Elizabeth established the Court of High Commission which, especially in the hands of Archbishop Whitgift, sought to ensure the enforcement of the royal will in ecclesiastical matters.

Although it was not Henry VIII's intention, his political reformation also raised the issue of whether the doctrine of the Catholic Church would be rejected along with papal authority. Those who favoured the doctrines of the continental reformers and those who wished to retain pre-Reformation teachings enjoyed their respective periods of ascendancy in the reigns of Edward VI and Mary. Elizabeth, like her father in his last years, seemed to favour a combination of Protestant doctrine, an ambiguous Prayer Book, and elements of conservative practice, which made up a Church acceptable to most of her subjects. Although she accepted a redefinition of her royal Supremacy, now recognised as 'Supreme Governor' rather than as 'Supreme Head', there can be little doubt that she took her political authority over the English Church every bit as seriously as her father had done.

Elizabeth's essentially political compromise seemed to many contemporaries to have few spiritual merits. The Church that even Bishop Jewel described as a 'leaden mediocrity' faced opposition from two angles: conservative opposition to the doctrine of her Church, and radical Protestant opposition to the hierarchy and discipline that the Queen wished to impose upon it. The ultimate survival of this hybrid Anglican Church has convinced some historians that the Elizabethan religious settlement was one of the great successes of the reign. The available evidence now suggests, however, that the official settlement may have been widely circumvented or ignored, and that its enforcement may have constituted one of the great failures of Tudor government.

ANALYSIS (1): TO WHAT EXTENT DID THE CROWN CONTROL THE ENGLISH CHURCH BEFORE THE HENRICIAN REFORMATION?

The nature of the English Reformation has been investigated more thoroughly in recent years than any other aspect of Tudor history. One major result of this investigation has been a lively debate about the health and vitality of orthodox religion in England in the early sixteenth century. By providing evidence that popular religion was healthy and thriving on the eve of the Reformation J.J. Scarisbrick (1) and Eamon Duffy (2) have strengthened the arguments of those historians who view that movement primarily as a 'revolution from above', as a governmental reform imposed upon a population with little other motive for change. This leads to one further question about the nature of the early Tudor Church. Contemporary kings of France and Spain dominated ecclesiastical affairs within their realms without a legislative break from Rome. Were such measures necessary in England because the English crown lacked practical control over the English Church in the first forty-five years of Tudor rule?

Recent writers have disagreed about the exact balance of power between Church and state in the early years of Tudor rule. Some, aware that the great break with Rome was only a few decades away, have attached substantial constitutional importance to Henry VII's relations with the Church. 'It was the first of the Tudors', John Guy (3) has argued, 'who transformed the relationship between civil and Church authorities. [He] could not tolerate vested interests incompatible with [his] secular aims: thus franchises were attacked, liberties suppressed.' Guy claims that the reign witnessed a concerted effort on the part of royal courts to undermine the independence of ecclesiastical courts by the use of *praemunire* proceedings, with the Attorney-General, Sir James Hobart, in the forefront of this movement. (4) Similarly, it has been argued that the King greatly increased his control over the English bishops, selecting them for potential or past services as royal administrators, rather than for their spirituality. It is certainly true that of twenty-seven bishops appointed by Henry VII, sixteen had degrees in law rather than in theology. It is equally true that Henry exercised the same forms of political control over his bishops as he exercised over his secular nobility, and several were forced to enter into recognisances with him as guarantees of their good behaviour (see Chapter 1). S.B. Chrimes believes that Henry VII was taking significant steps towards the events of the 1530s, noting that 'the very full measure of control over the episcopate attained by Henry VII may have constituted a condition precedent without which his son might well have been confronted with a far greater degree of opposition from the Church'. (5)

Many others, however, would agree with Christopher Haigh's conclusion that 'it is only from the warping perspective of the Reformation that Henry VII's treatment of the Church seems at all remarkable'. (6) Such historians have perceived the reign as the perfect illustration of a subtle compromise between what J.A.F. Thomson (7) has called 'the two masters of the English Church'. In his view papal authority was faithfully maintained and acknowledged by the secular rulers, except when the 'liberties of the Church' threatened the interests of the crown. Laws of sanctuary, for instance, were maintained by Henry VII with the proviso that they could not protect those guilty of treason. They were thus breached in 1486 to allow the arrest of Humphrey Stafford. Benefit of clergy, similarly, was modified by statutes passed in 1489 and 1491, but these were concerned only to ensure that those who claimed immunity from punishment in lay courts really were in holy orders. Bitterly though Reformation propagandists complained of papal taxation, its impact under the early Tudors seems to have been moderate. W.E. Lunt's estimate was that the English Church paid an average of 4,800 pounds per annum to Rome between 1485 and 1534, compared to a yearly average of 12,000 pounds to the crown. (8) In return for his acknowledgement of papal authority, Henry VII received virtually every political favour that he requested. A papal dispensation authorised his marriage to Elizabeth of York and legitimised the children of the marriage. His candidate and supporter, John Morton, was appointed Archbishop of Canterbury and eventually made a cardinal. A papal ruling deprived cathedral chapters of any meaningful role in the selection of bishops and left the matter entirely in the hands of the crown. Viewed from this perspective, the evidence supports A.G. Dickens's conclusion that 'the advent of the Tudor dynasty formed no landmark; the reign of Henry VII was far from presaging major crises in Anglo-papal or Church-State relations'. (9)

Dickens's conclusion might equally apply to the accession of Henry VIII. The political ascendancy of Thomas Wolsey probably marked the high point in this cooperation between crown and papacy, and provided the King with an unparalleled degree of control over the English Church. A.F. Pollard's interpretation, (10) that Wolsey exercised this authority in the interests of the papacy, in the hope of becoming Pope himself, is no longer widely accepted. Instead it appears much more likely that Wolsey acquired this degree of ecclesiastical authority because it was in the King's interests that he should do so. 'What has misled in the past', Peter Gwyn (11) has written, 'has been the concentration on Wolsey to the exclusion of his chief source of power, Henry VIII. In fact, it was his close association with the King, rather than his legatine powers, that enabled him so easily to dominate the English Church.' The unusual prolongation of Wolsey's powers as legate *a latere* was granted by the papacy at Henry's behest. It was granted because, threatened by both the King of France and the Holy Roman Emperor, successive Popes looked upon the King of England as a kindred spirit and a valuable support in a dangerous political environment. It was clearly to Henry's advantage that the legate's court, the most powerful Church court in the land, lay in the hands of his chief minister. 'Wolsey's churchmanship', Peter Gwyn concludes, 'should be seen as another aspect of his work as leading royal servant. As long as Henry felt that he could trust Wolsey, the legatine powers were an ideal solution to the problem of securing a subservient Church.' Gwyn also suggests that it was no coincidence that Wolsey gained such authority over the English Church immediately after the bitter controversy aroused by Hunne's Case (1514–15), in the course of which some churchmen, including the Archbishop of Canterbury, had made a determined stand on the issue of the liberties of the Church. Archbishop Warham subsequently complained that the extension of Wolsey's powers left him 'a shadow and image of an archbishop and legate, devoid of authority and jurisdiction', and this may very well have been Henry's intention. Wolsey was the personification of a compromise by which Henry dominated the English Church, but did so in theory through powers granted by the Church itself.

The Henrician Reformation took place, therefore, not because of the increasing incompatibility of papal and royal authority, but because a system, hitherto viable and effective, suddenly ceased to work. 'The very fact that so much had previously been given', writes Christopher Harper-Bill, (12) 'worsened the shock of rejection when, because of changed political circumstances in Italy, Clement VII was unable to expedite the annulment of Henry VIII's first marriage.' The time that elapsed between Henry's decision to divorce Catherine of Aragon, and the achievement of that divorce through English law suggests to many writers that for some time the King's advisers could see no alternative to a papal solution, and fully expected that solution to work in the end. The legislation of the 1530s clearly gave the crown powers that it did not previously possess, particularly in terms of the definition of doctrine, and access to the property of the Church. On the other hand, many of the earlier statutes, the Act in Restraint of Appeals, the Act in Restraint of Annates, and even perhaps the Act of Supremacy, served largely to provide a legal basis for powers that the crown had exercised informally for some time. What was new was that they were now based upon statute law rather than upon a 'gentleman's agreement' between King and Pope.

Questions

1. 'The Reformation Parliament did not create a royal supremacy over the English Church: it merely legalised and institutionalised a political dominance that had existed for at least fifty years.' To what extent do you agree with this statement?

2. Explain and assess the view that between 1485 and 1529 the English Church had 'two masters, one in England and one in Rome'.

ANALYSIS (2): HOW EFFECTIVELY WAS ELIZABETH'S GOVERNMENT ABLE TO ENFORCE ITS RELIGIOUS SETTLEMENT?

During the last fifty years the debate over the nature of the English Reformation has produced a number of distinct interpretations. These have differed mainly in the relative importance that they attach to Protestant enthusiasm among the population at large ('Reformation from below'), and to the role of government edicts forcing religious change upon an essentially conservative populace ('Reformation from above'). At the same time, historians have differed over the pace at which reformist ideas gained ground in England. If we accept, for instance, G.R. Elton's (13) judgement that 'by 1553 England was certainly nearer to being a Protestant country than to anything else', then we are likely to conclude that Mary's attempts to restore Catholicism were unrealistic and doomed to failure, and that it was a relatively easy task for Elizabeth and her ministers to implement their broadly Protestant settlement.

Recent research, however, has established a convincing consensus that religious conservatism remained strong in many localities and that it was no easy matter for Elizabeth's government to put its religious settlement into effect. Christopher Haigh (14) describes the settle-ment of 1559–63 as merely another in a succession of 'political reformations' and concludes that 'the Church of England was not immediately protestantised in its clergy, furnishings, services and the beliefs of its people [and that] the government did not dare to enforce the Elizabethan Settlement rigorously'. All that had happened by 1563 was that a burst of legislation 'gave England Protestant laws and made popular Protestantism possible'.

How easily were these Protestant laws enforced in a society that had recently accepted Mary's Counter-Reformation with equanimity? Ronald Hutton's research (15) into the removal of images and other outward signs of the 'old religion' suggests that this physical process was relatively easy: 'the machinery of coercion and supervision deployed by the government was so effective that for most parishes passive resistance was simply not an option'. The elimination of Catholic beliefs and practices, however, may have been much more difficult. The studies undertaken by A.G. Dickens (16) on recusancy (17) in Yorkshire led him to conclude that religious conservatism went through two distinct, and largely unconnected, phases. 'Survivalism', a conservative attachment to the practices of the pre-Reformation Church, faded steadily in the face of government action and was replaced in the 1580s, after the arrival of missionary priests from Douai, by a new brand of recusant Catholicism, with a narrower base, but a healthier ideological foundation. J.J. Scarisbrick (18) conveyed a similar impression when he wrote that on a national level in 1558–60, 'there was a large-scale collapse [of Catholic resistance] when Elizabeth put the old order to the test. The [Marian] bishops stood firm – but not many other people imitated them.' Further regional studies have produced a different picture. Christopher Haigh has challenged Professor Dickens's 'model' by showing that the recusancy of the 1580s and 1590s was often based upon a strong degree of Catholic resistance in the earlier decades, led by Marian priests and by Catholic laymen. 'It was the Marian clergy who initiated lay recusant Catholicism, which was already well established before the mission from the continent could have any real effect.' D.M. Palliser (19) has questioned the traditional picture of Catholicism folding before Elizabethan legislation by suggesting that the government simply did not have the means to impose its will upon powerful and concentrated local communities.

> Several recent studies suggest that visitation procedures could only cope with minority problems: if a group of offenders were generally supported by the other parishioners, they would be unlikely to be presented [i.e. reported to the authorities]. That suggests the depressing possibility that the records indicate only the distribution of small minorities of dissenters and that areas of widespread dissent might often pass unrecorded. (20)

The evidence now suggests overwhelmingly that the government and its agents failed to eliminate surviving Catholic practices in many localities in the 1560s. Historians remain undecided, however, whether this should be seen as the result of formidable obstacles in the path of determined reformers, or of cautious pragmatism on the part of a government that preferred peace to advanced Protestantism. Daunting obstacles certainly abounded. D.M. Palliser has stressed the sheer size of such dioceses as York, Lichfield and Norwich, and the unsuitability, both in terms of situation and of revenues, of the new (1541) diocese of Chester as a centre for the ecclesiastical government of Lancashire.

He also emphasises the reliance of both Queen and bishops upon 'unpaid officials in the localities' and upon 'the relationship of the bishop with the county community of nobles and gentry'. Even the ardent Bishop Sandys of Worcester found it hard to make headway against the local influence of Sir John Browne, formerly Queen Mary's Secretary of State. Yet we must also consider the possibility that the Queen did not wish the settlement to be vigorously enforced in cases where this might threaten local political stability. This was certainly the picture outlined many years ago by Sir John Neale, (21) and which has been confirmed more recently by Ralph Houlbrooke (22), who has stressed how much more advanced many of the new bishops were in their Protestantism than was the Queen herself. He cites the case of Bishop Curteys of Chichester, disciplined by the Council for his stand against conservative elements among the Sussex gentry. 'Bishops', he concludes, 'were expected to act as [the Council's] eyes and ears, but to avoid any action which might provoke controversy or stir local passions.'

Even if Catholic survivals in the 1560s may be interpreted as part of a successful government policy, the events of 1569–72 clearly marked a turning point. The Revolt of the Northern Earls, according to J.J. Scarisbrick, 'revealed to the government with shocking clarity how lamentably the new regime had failed to take root in the north-east', and the Pope's formal excommunication of Elizabeth further undermined any policy of compromise. After these crises the government certainly used its available machinery more vigorously to enforce observance. Although the incidence of recusancy appears to increase in the years that followed, this may only be because the government took a more urgent approach to the problem, and thus exposed more of it. The Bishops of Norwich, Chichester and Winchester were ordered by the Council to undertake visitations in 1569, and when the Bishop of Chester proved ineffective in this respect in south Lancashire (1571), a special metropolitan visitation was organised to do the job for him. Christopher Haigh also suggests that 'if the number of recusants really did increase in the 1570s this was partly because conformism became less attractive as the Protestant bishops drove conservative practices from the parish churches'. Although Catholic resistance was not fully overcome, Elizabeth's long reign provided time and opportunity for the effective establishment of a Protestant Church of England. By the 1580s, in Haigh's view, the government had effectively won the struggle at a national, if not always at a local level: 'With each age-cohort, Protestants gained a higher proportion of the positions of power, until they controlled the Privy Council, the Court, Parliament, county commissions of the peace, and civic governments, and were well on the way to control of churches and schools.'

Elizabeth faced a quite different set of problems over the control of her more enthusiastic Protestant subjects. Although Elizabeth's personal religious views remain obscure, there can be little serious doubt that she attached great importance to the maintenance of her own authority as 'Supreme Governor' and that she remained implacably hostile to the independent modes of thought that characterised the puritan movement. Many of the Protestant bishops that she was forced to appoint at the beginning of her reign did not share these priorities. Rosemary O'Day (23) notes that 'the first generation of Elizabethan bishops had one thing in common: they did not accept for one moment that the initial Elizabethan religious "settlement" was a settlement at all. Many accepted sees in the first place because they wanted to be able to shape the Church from within according to the guidelines of the continental reformed churches.' Such writers portray an extremely energetic episcopate, more concerned in the first twenty years of the reign with the promotion of 'godliness' and the suppression of 'superstition' than with the strict enforcement of the religious settlement. This clash of priorities culminated in 1576–77, when Archbishop Grindal was ordered by the Queen to suppress 'prophesyings', meetings at which the scriptures were explained and interpreted to clergymen and laity. His refusal to do so, and his suggestion that the Queen lacked the religious authority to make such a request, led to his suspension from office for the rest of his life. In terms of the royal Supremacy, such defiance marked a turning point, for as Claire Cross (24) notes, 'the Queen appears to have taken greater care from this date that no cleric with the known independence of Grindal should be elevated to the episcopate'. John Whitgift's appointment as Archbishop of Canterbury (1583) clearly symbolises this policy, yet it did not solve the Queen's problems altogether. Archbishop Sandys (York) and Bishop Chaderton (Chester) both introduced such 'exercises' to combat conservatism in the north after the Queen's veto.

Elizabeth's difficulties in this respect extended far beyond these leading clergymen. Claire Cross has emphasised the role played by Protestant laymen who used their local patronage to appoint clergy whose religious views coincided with their own, rather than with those expressed in the official settlement.

At Westminster the Queen acted as though she were the untrammelled head of the Church; in the localities the nobility and gentry, even certain town corporations, assuming without question that some share in the direction of the Church belonged to them as the governing elite, went ahead with the reformation of the local church.

Rosemary O'Day and Patrick Collinson (25) have also shown how the Queen's wishes were often obstructed by the influence and patronage of some of her own leading courtiers. Men such as Leicester, Bedford and Pembroke had sufficient sympathy with moderate puritanism and sufficient influence over church appointments often to frustrate Whitgift's conservative intentions. Such obstacles may have been reduced in the last decade of the reign, with the death of many such noble patrons, but Claire Cross has emphasised the problems that this 'triumph of conservatism' caused in the longer term.

> Whereas Grindal had consciously tried to lead his clergy like a primitive pastor, Whitgift treated his delinquent ministers as though they were errant scholars. Resentment flared up anew against persecuting prelates and encouraged the growth of hostility to episcopacy as such.

Besides, such changes at Court did little to alter the problems that Elizabeth and Whitgift faced in the localities, in terms both of puritan and of Catholic nonconformity. There now exists a broad consensus among historians that the Queen won the political battle over the religious settlement, successfully resisting parliamentary and extra-parliamentary attempts from both religious extremes to alter it. Beyond the centre of government, however, a different picture emerges. 'In the last resort,' Claire Cross has concluded, 'the state failed to compel the laity into uniformity because the zealots, both Catholic and Protestant, disregarding the parish system, made their own households into centres of evangelism. There the Elizabethan state had not the power to intrude.'

Questions

1. How far do you agree with the claim that 'Elizabeth's royal supremacy over the English Church was largely theoretical'?
2. 'Under Elizabeth, English bishops became effective agents of the government's ecclesiastical policy.' Do you agree?

SOURCES

1. RELATIONS BETWEEN THE CROWN AND THE CHURCH

Source A: from a bull of Pope Innocent VIII for publication in the Province of Canterbury, 1490.

Our Holy Father Pope Innocent VIII. Of his proper motion without any procurement of our sovereign lord the King or of any other person: for conservation of the universal peace, understanding the long and grievous variance and debates that have been in this realm of England between the house of the duchy of Lancaster and the house of the duchy of York, willing all such divisions in time following to be put apart by the counsel and consent of his college of cardinals, approveth, confirmeth and establisheth the matrimony and conjunction made between our sovereign lord King Henry VII of the house of Lancaster and the noble princess Elizabeth of the house of York, with all their issue lawfully born between the same.

Source B: an extract from *The Great Chronicle of London*, describing trials held in the aftermath of the Stanley Conspiracy in 1495.

Upon the 29th day of January was holden within the Guildhall an *oyer determiner* before the Mayor and other commissioners of the King's Council. Where upon the first day inquiries were made upon these persons as follows: first the Dean of St Paul's, the Provincial of the Black Friars, the Prior of Langley, the parson of St Stephen's in Walbrook [and eight laymen]. The 30th day of January were cast and deemed [judged] to be hanged, drawn and quartered the aforenamed Dean of Paul's, the Provincial of the Black Friars, an excellent divine and one of the most famous preachers of that time about London, and the Prior of Langley aforesaid. The which three persons the King of his gracious goodness after a certain time of imprisonment pardoned and acquitted.

Source C: from a letter written by the Milanese ambassador in England to Ludovico Sforza, ruler of Milan, September 1497.

The Pope is entitled to much praise, for he loves the King cordially, and strengthens his power by ecclesiastical censures, so that at all times rebels are excommunicated. The efficacy of these censures is now felt by the Cornishmen, who are in this trouble that all who eat grain garnered since the rebellion, or drink beer brewed with this year's crops, die as if they had taken poison, and hence it is publicly reported that the King is under the direct protection of Almighty God.

Source D: from the records of the Convocation of Canterbury, January–February 1489.

On 19th January there entered the chapter house John Dynham, Treasurer of England, John, Earl of Oxford, Thomas, Earl of Derby and others of the King's Council, sent by the King. The Treasurer elegantly explained that the King was enormously grateful for the charity and the concern that they had shown for his Majesty and the honour of his realm, and asked for their perseverance in this, promising to be a willing defender of the rights and the liberties of the Church in England. He then announced that the King, partly because of the request of the community of the realm expressed in the present Parliament, partly and more especially to counter the threat posed to the realm by the King of France, needed the succour of the prelates and the clergy of the province, not only their prayers but their financial aid.

On 27th February, in the archbishop's presence, was granted to the King, in the name of all the clergy, a great subsidy of 25,000 pounds, to be paid in two instalments.

Source E: part of a speech delivered by Henry VIII at Baynard's Castle in London, in 1515. In the speech, Henry refuses to refer Hunne's Case, with its implications for the authority of common and canon law, to Rome for judgement.

By the ordinance and sufferance of God we are King of England. And the kings of England in time past have never had any superior but God alone. Wherefore know you well that we shall maintain the right of our crown and of our temporal jurisdiction as well in this point as in all others.

Source F: from the oath of fealty taken by Charles Booth upon his enthronement as Bishop of Hereford, April 1516.

I renounce and utterly forsake all manner of words and sentences contained in the Pope's Bull granted to me of the bishopric of Hereford which be or in any wise may be prejudicial to your Highness, to your crown or dignity royal, and therefore I put me wholly in your grace, beseeching the same to have restitution of the temporalities of my said bishopric which I claim to hold of your Grace. And also I shall be faithful and true, and faith and troth I shall bear unto you, sovereign lord Henry, by the grace of God King of England and France and lord of Ireland. I shall be obeisant [obedient], and if anything I know prejudicial or hurtful to your person or estate, I shall resist it to the best of my power or give thereof knowledge to your Highness or to such of your Council as shall give your Grace knowledge thereof, with all the diligence that may goodly be done. So help me God and the Holy Gospels.

Source G: from the Act in Restraint of Appeals, 1533.

Where by sundry, old authentic histories and chronicles, it is manifestly declared and expressed that this realm of England is an empire, governed by one supreme head and king, having the dignity and royal estate of the imperial crown, unto whom a state, comprising all sorts of degrees of people, owes next to God, a humble and natural obedience. The King is also instituted and furnished by the goodness and consent of Almighty God with whole, entire power. He can thus render and yield justice and final determination of legal cases for all manner of folk within this realm, in all cases, matters and debates, without interference from any foreign princes or potentates.

Questions

1. Explain the following references which occur in the sources: 'an *oyer determiner* before . . . the King's Council' (Source B); 'the Cornishmen, who are in this trouble . . . since the rebellion' (Source C); 'temporal jurisdiction' (Source E).
*2. Assess the reliability and the value of Sources A and C as evidence of the relationship between Henry VII and the papacy.
3. On the strength of the evidence contained in Sources A, C and D, summarise the political benefits that Henry VII derived from the support of the papacy.
4. 'The principles put forward in the Act in Restraint of Appeals represented a significant change in the relationship between the English crown and the papacy.' How far is this statement supported by the evidence contained in these sources?

Worked answer

*2. [The question requires the student not only to understand the content of the documents but, by drawing conclusions about their origin and purpose, to judge their accuracy and their value to the historian. It should also help the student to appreciate that a document that is not entirely accurate may nevertheless have considerable illustrative value for the historian.]

Dealing first with the reliability of the documents, it is evident that the facts reported in Source C are inaccurate. Common sense tells us that God did not strike Cornishmen dead because of their recent rebellion against Henry VII. The unreliability of Source A is more difficult to detect. Much of the bull is a simple statement of fact, that Innocent

VIII did indeed give his blessing to the marriage between Henry and Elizabeth of York. The bull is misleading, on the other hand, in its suggestion that he did so 'of his proper motion without any procurement of our sovereign lord the King'. Our background knowledge of the period tells us that this was a political favour sought by Henry in order to enhance his prestige and authority within the realm, and in order to secure the succession of his heirs. We cannot accept, therefore, the suggestion in the sources that the Pope extended an almost miraculous protection over Henry VII of his own free will.

This does not mean, however, that the documents are without value to the historian. On the contrary, they provide valuable evidence of the success of Henry's relations with the Church. The misleading section in Source A, for instance, illustrates that Henry was at pains to give the impression that his marriage and the Tudor succession had the unsolicited blessing of God's representative on earth. Source C provides the historian with valuable evidence of the success of Henry's policy. Given that it was the duty of the ambassador to send reliable news, rather than idle gossip, to his master, the document illustrates that a section of informed popular opinion truly believed that Henry was 'under the direct protection of Almighty God' and indeed that so well-informed and circumspect an individual as the Milanese ambassador believed it himself.

SOURCES

2. THE ENFORCEMENT OF THE ELIZABETHAN RELIGIOUS SETTLEMENT

Source H: part of the Act of Uniformity, 1559.

From and after the feast of the Nativity of St John Baptist next coming, all and every person and persons inhabiting within this realm or any other the Queen's Majesty's dominions, shall diligently and faithfully, having no lawful or reasonable excuse to be absent, endeavour themselves to resort to their parish church or chapel accustomed, or upon reasonable let thereof to some usual place where common prayer and such service of God shall be used. And then and there to abide orderly and soberly during the time of the common prayer, preachings or other service of God there to be used and ministered; upon pain of punishment by the censures of the Church, and also upon pain that every person so offending shall forfeit for every such offence twelve pence.

Source I: from the confession of a participant in the Revolt of the Northern Earls, 1569, dated April 1570.

William Blenkinsop, minor canon, aged sixty five. He was at the cathedral [at Durham] on St Andrew's Day. Robert Peirson said mass at the high altar. The Earl of Northumberland coming to Durham the Saturday next after, William Holmes preached on the Sunday next after, and he spoke expressedly against the state of religion established in England, commending the late service that was abolished, and affirming that he had authority to reconcile men to the Church of Rome; and willed all that were disposed to be reconciled to kneel down; whereupon he pronounced a form of absolution in Latin, in the name of Christ's bishop, Pius, of Rome.

Source J: from a report by Bishop Barlow of Chichester on the state of religion in his diocese, 1569.

In the church of Arundel, certain altars do stand yet still to the offence of the godly, which murmur and speak much against the same. They have yet in the diocese, in many places, images hidden up and other popish ornaments, ready to set up the mass again within twenty four hours' warning; as in the town of Battle and in the parish of Lindfield, where they be yet very blind and superstitious. In the town of Battle, when the preacher does come and speak against the Pope's doctrine, they will not abide but get them out of the church. The schoolmaster is the cause of their going out, who afterwards in corners among the people does gainsay the preachers. In some places, many bring to church the old popish Latin primers, and use to pray upon them all the time when the lessons are being read and in the time of the litany.

Source K: from a report to the Privy Council on the state of religion in Lancashire and Cheshire, 1591.

Small reformation has been made there by the Ecclesiastical Commission, as may appear by the emptiness of churches on Sundays. The youth for the most part are trained up by such as profess papistry; no examination is had of schools and schoolmasters. The proclamation for the apprehension of seminarists, Jesuits and mass priests is not executed, nor are their Lordships' letters commanding the justices to call before them quarterly all parsons, vicars, curates, churchwardens and sworn men, and examine them on how the statutes of 1 and 23 Eliz. as to resorting to churches are obeyed. Some of the coroners and justices do not frequent church, and many of them have not communicated at the Lord's supper since the beginning of Her Majesty's reign.

Source L: from a letter written by the Bishop of Peterborough to Lord Burghley, complaining of Protestant nonconformity in his diocese, 1573.

In the town of Overton where Mr Carlton dwelleth there is no divine service upon most Sundays according to the Book of Common Prayer, but instead thereof two sermons. When they are determined to receive the communion, they repair to Whiston where it is their joy to have many out of divers parishes there to receive the sacraments with preachers and ministers to their own liking, and contrary to the form prescribed by the public order of the realm. In their ways they be very bold and stout, like men that seem not to be without great friends.

Source M: from a letter from Archbishop Grindal to the Queen on the subject of preaching and prophesyings, December 1576.

Concerning the learned exercises and conference among the ministers of the Church: I have consulted with divers of my brethren the bishops, by letters, who think the same as I do: a thing profitable to the Church, and therefore expedient to be continued. The said exercises, for the interpretation and exposition of the scriptures are both profitable to increase knowledge among the ministers, and tendeth to the edifying of the hearers.

And now having been so long and tedious with your Majesty, I will draw to an end, most humbly praying the same well to consider these two short petitions following.

The first is that you will refer all these ecclesiastical matters which toucheth religion, or the doctrine and discipline of the Church, to the bishops and divines of your realm.

The second petition that I have to make to your Majesty is this: that when you deal in matters of faith and religion, you would not use to pronounce so resolutely and peremptorily, as from authority, but always remember that in God's causes the will of God, and not the will of any earthly creature, is to take place. It is the antichristian voice of the pope, 'So I will have it; so I command; let my will stand for a reason.' Remember, Madam, that you are a mortal creature.

Source N: the Three Articles of Archbishop Whitgift, 1583.

That none be permitted to preach, read, catechize, minister the sacraments, or execute any other ecclesiastical function, unless he consent and subscribe to these Articles following: 1. That her Majesty, under God, hath, and ought to have, the sovereignty and rule over all manner of persons born within her realms, either ecclesiastical or temporal.

2. That the Book of Common Prayer, and of ordering [ordaining] bishops, priests and deacons, containeth in it nothing contrary to the word of God, and

that he himself will use the form of the said book prescribed in public prayer and administration of the sacraments, and none other.

3. That he alloweth the book of [39] Articles, agreed upon by the archbishops and bishops of both provinces, and the whole clergy in the Convocation holden in London in the year of our Lord God 1562, and that he believeth all the Articles therein contained to be agreeable to the word of God.

Questions

1. Explain the following references that appear in these sources: 'seminarists, Jesuits and mass priests' (Source K); 'men that seem not to be without great friends' (Source L); 'the book of [39] Articles' (Source N).
2. Compare the forms of Catholic nonconformity illustrated by Sources I, J and K.
3. What do you deduce from Sources M and N about the different priorities of Grindal and Whitgift as Archbishops of Canterbury?
*4. What evidence is there in these sources about the effectiveness of Elizabeth's bishops as agents for the enforcement of her religious settlement?
5. 'In Elizabeth's reign the government lacked the means to enforce its religious policy in the localities.' How far do these sources, and other evidence known to you, lead you to agree with this statement?

Worked answer

*4. [The student will approach this question with some background knowledge of the role that Elizabeth's bishops were required to play in the enforcement of her religious settlement. It requires them to test that knowledge against the evidence that they find in the documents themselves. As the question may be answered in different degrees of depth, it is important that the student should resist the temptation to be satisfied with a simple answer, but should sift the sources in order to extract all the relevant evidence that they contain.]

It is immediately obvious that several of the sources deal with failures to enforce the terms of the religious settlement. Sources J and L are both written by bishops, reporting instances of non-conformity within their dioceses. While Bishop Barlow was struggling to eliminate Catholic survivals in Sussex, the Bishop of Peterborough was helpless to prevent Protestant nonconformity in his own see. Although Source K is not necessarily written by a bishop, it does specifically refer to the failure of an episcopal agency, the Ecclesiastical Commission, to root out practising Catholics in Lancashire and Cheshire. It is also significant that all three of these sources were written more than a decade after Elizabeth's succession, and that the settlement was thirty years old when Source K was written, in 1591.

The documents provide plenty of evidence of the role that the ecclesiastical hierarchy was *supposed* to play. In Source N the Archbishop of Canterbury lays down very clearly the orthodoxy that was expected of all clergymen within the Church of England, which his bishops are expected to enforce. In Sources J and L, by reporting frankly upon the local state of religion, the Bishops of Chichester and Peterborough are indeed playing their role as the 'eyes and ears' of central government. The sources also supply much information about the local obstacles that frustrated the bishops. We find references to the conservatism of local magistrates (Source K), the influence of local gentry and nobility (Source L), and that of lesser figures such as the local schoolmaster (Source J). Source I provides the most spectacular example of a local magnate in opposition to the settlement, although the 1569 rising was an isolated and sensational example of such opposition.

Finally, Source M illustrates that, in some particulars, even so prominent a churchman as Elizabeth's own Archbishop of Canterbury could not be relied upon to enforce the Queen's wishes. Although Grindal would certainly have shared the regrets expressed by his colleague in Chichester about the survival of Catholic practices, he favours the advance of 'godly' Protestantism, refuses to accept the Queen's opposition to 'prophesyings', and even challenges her authority to ban them. Source M, therefore, illustrates the fact that, in terms of Protestant nonconformity, some of Elizabeth's most eminent ecclesiastical servants actually had an agenda different from her own.

8

FINANCE

BACKGROUND NARRATIVE

The finances of the Tudor crown fell into two broad categories.
'Ordinary' income derived primarily from the monarch's landed
property, in the form of rents and other payments like those of any
other great landlord. The extent of the crown lands was a matter of
central importance to royal government, and the first two Tudors
provided the dynasty with a firm basis in this respect. Henry
VII's combination of the lands of the Duchy of Lancaster with
those of the House of York was enhanced by the lands acquired
through attainders and the deaths of royal relatives. His son's
wholesale acquisition of church lands through the dissolution of
the monasteries placed the English crown in a position of unprecedented strength. On the other hand, gifts of land to royal servants
or, more commonly, the sale of lands to fund major political projects
such as military campaigns, could weaken the crown considerably.

Certain other forms of income, such as the profits of wardship,
were associated with landed income, because they derived from
the monarch's status as a great feudal lord. As such, he or she was
entitled to protect the person and to administer the lands of the
underage heir of any feudal tenant. The complexities of identifying
wards and collecting money from this source caused the crown to
create a separate administrative system to deal with this income. The
Master of Wards performed this role until the creation (1540) of
a distinct Court of Wards and Liveries. The crown also had access to
other, variable sources of income granted to it for the defence and

administration of the realm. Most important of these were the customs duties (tunnage and poundage) usually voted to the monarch for life in the first Parliament of the reign. The crown was also entitled to receive 'fruits of justice', the sums raised by fines and confiscations in the law courts, and had access to the income of church offices, especially bishoprics, when a diocese stood vacant between the death of one bishop and the appointment of the next.

The second financial category, the crown's 'extraordinary' income, was that granted by Parliament in the form of taxation in response to special needs. The most obvious and most frequent of these was war, which also constituted the largest item of royal expenditure, particularly during the reign of Henry VIII and in the last fifteen years of Elizabeth's reign. In peacetime, the major elements of royal expenditure were likely to be the maintenance of the royal Court and household, building projects or gifts to reward loyal servants.

The machinery which handled these finances underwent a number of changes, mainly in the first half of the Tudor period. The Exchequer, traditionally the crown's main agency for the receipt and accounting of royal income, survived this period as a major financial institution. Others grew around it, however, to meet the immediate needs of the monarchy. Henry VII made greater use of certain institutions of the royal Court and Household, notably the Royal Chamber and the Jewel House, particularly because of their convenience in making ready cash available to the King. In subsequent reigns, the Privy Chamber played an increasingly important role in the handling of the crown's cash. New sources of royal income gave rise to new institutions. Thus, in Henry VIII's reign, the vast increase in royal revenue derived from the confiscation of church lands caused extensive administrative reform. The Court of Augmentations (1536) was established to deal with the crown's income from former monastic lands, while the Court of First Fruits and Tenths (1540) handled clerical payments that had previously been due to the papacy. By the reign of Edward VI the crown's income was handled by at least ten different offices, and rationalisation became the order of the day. The Court of Augmentations absorbed the Court of General Surveyors (1547), and this and other financial bodies were absorbed into the Exchequer during Mary's reign. Throughout, these changes owed much less to long-term planning, than to the immediate needs of the crown in response to particular circumstances.

ANALYSIS (1): CAN EITHER WOLSEY OR CROMWELL BE SAID TO HAVE SOLVED THE FINANCIAL PROBLEMS OF THE ENGLISH CROWN?

There is broad agreement among historians that Henry VIII inherited from his father a financial system able to cope in all respects with the normal demands of English government. This healthy situation was transformed, however, by the young King's decision to go to war in the opening years of his reign. 'It was by his active foreign policy,' wrote F.C. Dietz (1), 'and his participation in two wars with France [1511–14 and 1522–25] which he espoused with the enthusiasm of a reckless boy, that the revenue system as perfected by Henry VII was rendered inadequate.' It was a primary task of his successive chief ministers, Thomas Wolsey and Thomas Cromwell, to find the means to finance such ambitious enterprises.

For many years Wolsey's effectiveness as a provider of finance for Henry's ambitious foreign policies was judged in the context of the reforms undertaken in the 1530s by Thomas Cromwell. In this respect, as in others, Wolsey was regarded as energetic in his exploitation of traditional sources of income, while his more imaginative successor revolutionised the very bases of royal income. Recent authorities are more willing to judge the Cardinal in the context of his own time and of the specific demands that he faced. Peter Gwyn (2) argues that if Wolsey was not an innovator, it was because circumstances did not demand innovation. His judgement that 'there is no reason to suppose that in similar circumstances [to those faced by Cromwell] Wolsey would not have risen to the challenge' is an echo of that passed many years ago by F.C. Dietz: 'He did nothing which indicates that he saw that the normal royal revenues would have to be vastly increased in the not far distant future. But even the greatest statesmen seldom cross bridges until they come to them.'

Some recent authorities have, in any case, been inclined to regard Wolsey as an innovator in his own right. His use of the subsidy as a prime source of parliamentary taxation is often seen as a major advance. John Guy (3) is inclined to credit Wolsey with the development of the subsidy and stresses its advanced nature:

Unlike the French *taille* or *gabelle*, or the poll tax and fifteenths and tenths which the subsidy increasingly superseded, Wolsey's system of taxation was progressive as well as efficient. For the first time since 1334 the crown was levying taxation which accurately reflected the true wealth of tax-payers.

Richard Hoyle (4) also attaches great importance to the 'military surveys' undertaken in 1522 to gain information about individual wealth within the realm, and which served as a basis for the 'loans' requested by the crown in 1522–23. Whether such methods were original or not, it cannot be denied that Wolsey extracted unparalleled sums from the sources available. Important measures of retrenchment, such as the cancellation of various crown grants in the 1515 Act of Resumption, and the reform of the royal Household in the Ordinances of Eltham (1526), were overshadowed by an unparalleled tax yield. The 'loans' imposed in 1522 and 1523 were followed by the demands made of Parliament in 1523. Although Wolsey's critics have made much of his apparent confrontation with this assembly, Peter Gwyn is eager to stress that 'the Parliament of 1523 was an extremely successful one, at least from the crown's point of view. From it the King received an unprecedentedly large amount of money.'

Yet 1523 marked the high point of Wolsey's taxation policy. When the defeat of Francis I at Pavia (1525) tempted Henry to launch an invasion of France, his chief minister resorted to further arbitrary taxation, in the shape of the so-called 'Amicable Grant', to fund the project. When protests and potential rebellion persuaded Henry to abandon both the grant and the invasion, it became clear that the government had exhausted the potential of conventional taxation. Although the failure of the Amicable Grant has sometimes been seen as the first stage in the decline of Wolsey's influence, his fall cannot be ascribed to his financial policies. It remains open to question, therefore, how he should be judged as a finance minister. F.C. Dietz concluded that 'the financial situation was not serious or critical on Wolsey's fall', and that major problems arose subsequently with Henry's decision to undertake expensive building projects and to fortify Dover and Calais at great expense. David Starkey, (5) on the other hand, has judged that the situation was less stable than it appeared on the surface, so greatly did royal solvency depend upon the unpredictable source of the pension paid by Francis I.

Thomas Cromwell built upon Wolsey's experience, establishing the important principle of peacetime taxation in his Subsidy Act of 1534.

Yet he clearly appreciated the need for new solutions to the crown's financial problems. His major response, of course, was to exploit the property of the Church for the crown's benefit. Thus, although the measures envisaged in his state paper of 1534, for the wholesale confiscation of church property and the establishment of a salaried clergy, were never realised, ecclesiastical wealth was tapped by other means. Although Cromwell's early measures are commonly interpreted as a means of placing pressure upon the Church to annul Henry's marriage, historians specialising in financial matters have sometimes seen them as ends in themselves. F.C. Dietz argues that Cromwell's primary concern in the early and mid-1530s was the re-endowment of the crown, and that the threats of *praemunire* proceedings brought against the English Church were the first step in his plans to transfer ecclesiastical wealth to the state. It was a policy which culminated spectacularly in the dissolution of the English monasteries between 1536 and 1539.

Was the dissolution of the monasteries a success? In the short term it undoubtedly brought the crown far greater wealth than could ever have been derived from taxation, a probable total of 1.3 million pounds between 1536 and 1547. Any further judgement depends upon whether the dissolution is viewed as a long-term project or a short-term expedient. Historians have traditionally assumed that Cromwell aimed to benefit the crown in the long term. John Guy has recently raised the possibility, however, that 'there was a fundamental disjunction between Henry VIII's fiscal objectives and Cromwell's. The King's aim was to accumulate a war chest in the King's coffers. Cromwell's aim by contrast was that the proceeds of the dissolution should be used to create a permanent landed endowment for the "imperial" crown.' Either way, it is hard to avoid the conclusion that the dissolution constituted a 'failed revolution'. The crown had begun to sell off its monastic 'endowment' for ready cash by the time of Cromwell's fall (1540), and had disposed of as much as two-thirds of the land by Henry's death. Even so, such measures were insufficient to fund the wars fought in the 1540s. Richard Hoyle's survey of those campaigns reveals the extent to which the government returned to the sources exploited by Wolsey in the 1520s. It gained much of its finance from lay taxation (900,000 pounds between 1542 and 1552), loans (1542), subsidies (1543), clerical subsidies (1543, 1545 and 1548) and 'an emergency grant, except that in 1545 it was called a Benevolence and not an Amicable Grant'. Even when augmented by further sales of monastic lands these resources were insufficient and the crown resorted to the most damaging expedient of all. C.E. Challis (6) has estimated that, between

1542 and 1551, the crown derived 1.27 million pounds from the disastrous expedient of debasing the currency. It was a decision from which royal finances in the sixteenth century never recovered. However energetic and imaginative the work of these two great ministers was, they failed ultimately to provide an unrealistic monarch with the income that he required for his policies. Richard Hoyle makes this clear in his judgement that, for all their efforts, the 1540s 'saw the pattern of English monarchy established for the future: relatively poor in its resources, necessarily frugal, unable to fight foreign wars without taxation and obliged to balance its books by the sale of crown lands'.

Questions

1. 'So far from earning blame for a conservative financial policy, Thomas Wolsey deserves credit for so nearly satisfying the impossible demands of his royal master.' To what extent would you support this statement?
2. What, if anything, was new about the methods employed by Thomas Cromwell in the 1530s to finance the English crown?

ANALYSIS (2): WERE THE FINANCES OF THE CROWN ANY HEALTHIER AT THE END OF ELIZABETH'S REIGN THAN AT THE BEGINNING?

For many years the traditional view of Elizabeth's financial and political inheritance was that expressed by her contemporary, Armagil Waad, in his *Distresses of the Commonwealth* (1558): 'the Queen poor, the realm exhausted, the nobility poor and decayed. War with France and Scotland. The French king bestriding the realm, having one foot in Calais and the other in Scotland.' More recent analysis of government financial policies between 1550 and 1558, however, has suggested a much healthier picture. 'Fortunately,' writes D.M. Palliser, (7) 'both Northumberland and Mary kept the realm generally at peace and managed, with the aid of Lord Treasurer Winchester, to reduce expenditure and to increase income.' Winchester's masterpiece was the revision of the Book of Rates, which increased crown income from customs duties from 29,000 pounds in 1556–57 to 83,000 pounds in the first year of the new reign. Although Elizabeth now appears to have been fortunate in her financial inheritance, she also deserves credit for consolidating the progress of the 1550s. In particular, contemporaries were impressed by the continuing rebasement of the coinage. If modern historians don't quite accept Camden's judgement that this was 'her greatest glory', they largely concur with Palliser's conclusion that 'her revaluation did much for England's international standing [and] was also a domestic success, if judged by its effectiveness and permanence'.

After this early burst of fiscal activity, however, Elizabethan crown finances settled into a characteristically conservative 'rut'. The Queen and her ministers contented themselves with existing sources of income and made little effort to maximise the sums that were derived from them. Income from all sources of ordinary revenue increased by about 50 per cent in the course of the reign, scarcely keeping pace with inflation. Income from customs dues, boosted by the Marian reforms, only increased to 96,000 pounds per annum by the end of the reign, and no further attempt was made to revise the rates. Rents from crown lands rose only by about 25 per cent, partly as the result of land sales, but also due to the failure to make realistic assessments of the value of royal estates. 'There was clearly scope for very substantial increases during the Elizabethan period,' writes A.G.R. Smith (8), 'and Burghley's and the Queen's failure to take action, at a time when private landlords were sharply increasing their rentals, cost the government a great deal of much needed revenue.'

Nothing in recent research has altered the view that crown finances under Elizabeth were conservative and unimaginative in terms both of personnel and of machinery. The reign was dominated by two Lord Treasurers, Winchester (1550–72) and Burghley (1572–98), and in their hands the post became a major office of state. Winchester, although undoubtedly, in the words of A.G.R. Smith, 'one of the great administrators of Tudor England', was in his seventies by the time of Elizabeth's accession. Short-sighted, and famous for the illegibility of his handwriting, he was well past his best. Much more disappointing is the fact that Burghley showed less distinction as a financial administrator than in any other area of his work as Elizabeth's chief minister. His most enthusiastic biographer, Conyers Read (9), is forced to admit that 'he accepted the existing system as it was [and] never attempted any fundamental reform'. His record as Master of the Court of Wards (1561–98) was particularly poor. His failure to increase the crown's income from that source contrasts starkly with the achievement of his son and successor. Robert Cecil immediately raised the selling price of wardships by more than three times, and had trebled annual income by his death in 1612.

Similarly, the reign saw little institutional reform, in contrast to the thirty years that preceded it. Much work remains to be done on the financial machinery in the second half of the century, but the research of J.D. Alsop (10) on the Exchequer has sketched an unpromising picture. He portrays an institution 'staffed by a large body of reasonably capable and responsible administrators', yet so handicapped by inherited offices, personal disputes, and ignorance on the part of its political superiors, that it could not respond well to changing circumstances in the latter years of the reign. 'The Exchequer was adrift,' Alsop concludes, 'moving where the currents of economic change [and] vested interests would take it. [It] was very much in danger over the long term of becoming more closely associated with the problems of government than with their solution.'

While there is little dispute about the institutional conservatism and the static income of the reign, there is much less agreement among historians as to the overall political success of such policies. It has been argued in defence of Elizabeth and Burghley that for many years they had no need to innovate. Until the early 1580s, the greatest financial strength of Elizabeth's administration was its very low level of expenditure, and many commentators have seen this as a positive achievement. Conrad Russell (11) refers to Elizabeth's 'heroic decision to live within the royal income', and A.G.R. Smith concludes that 'it was largely due to the personal and unremitting vigilance of the Queen that England escaped financial disaster'. After all, the English crown remained solvent, while those of France and Spain were plagued by bankruptcy. Palliser also argues that financial conservatism and 'administrative inertia' were the price that the government chose to pay for political stability. Grants of crown lands may have served as a means of rewarding royal servants without increasing their salaries: failure to revise customs duties may have owed something to the desire not to alienate merchants at a time of considerable trading difficulties. Others have argued that this policy of low expenditure created serious problems in the longer term. The Queen certainly developed a reputation for extreme meanness when it came to rewarding her servants. Lawrence Stone (12) has stressed how the limitation of the crown's patronage gave rise to corruption as courtiers tried to make good the shortfall by 'accepting larger and larger gratuities, which soon became indistinguishable from bribes'. Some commentators have interpreted James I's profligate use of royal money as a distinct and deliberate reaction against the miserliness that royal servants had experienced at the hands of his predecessor. Conrad Russell stresses the use made of royal progresses to save money, and the low level of salaries paid to ambassadors. Elizabeth became something of an expert at patronage at little or no cost to herself; the most dramatic example of the political tensions that this could cause came in the last years of the reign with the parliamentary controversy over the trading monopolies that she had granted.

In the 1570s, Christopher Haigh (13) has concluded, such a 'hand to mouth' existence 'had worked well, because it had not been tested: from 1585, it was'. The war with Spain put the most serious strains upon the crown's financial system, and thus upon the political system of the state. The burden of parliamentary taxation, for example, was huge and unprecedented. Whereas Parliament had yielded only six subsidies in the period 1559–84, it now paid a subsidy in 1587, a double subsidy in 1589, triple subsidies in 1593 and 1597, and a quadruple subsidy in 1601. These were supplemented by benevolences from office-holders (1594 and 1599) and by forced loans (1588, 1590 and 1597). Even then, the system of taxation proved to be inadequate due to the laxity of earlier years. Because wealthy men had steadily lowered their own tax assessments, and because local commissioners used tax assessment as a form of patronage, under-assessing their friends and protégés, the tax yield was insufficient. The only way to meet the needs of the war was through further sales of crown lands.

Overall, the war, and the reign as a whole, do not seem to have left the crown with insuperable accounting problems. It is widely regarded as a remarkable achievement that, even after eighteen years of warfare, Elizabeth owed only 350,000 pounds at her death, a debt that could be cleared by income and subsidy within a year. She may, on the other hand, have bequeathed to the Stuarts political problems of a more complex and serious nature. If James I did not inherit a crippling debt, nor did he inherit the means to increase his income without controversy. As A.G.R. Smith has pointed out, Elizabeth's reign had 'accustomed the landed and trading classes to a situation in which they paid a very small part of their income in taxation. When they were called upon to give more under the early Stuarts their reluctance and resentments caused major difficulties for the crown.' Financial conservatism, in short, may have made a major contribution to the stability of Elizabeth's reign, while making an equally significant contribution to the instability of those that followed. In this respect, as in others, 'her conservatism, which had served England well for so many years was, at the end of her reign, a liability'.

Questions

1. In what ways, and with what success, did Elizabeth's government cope with the expense of war with Spain?

2. Was it ever realistic in the sixteenth century to expect the English crown to finance its policies from its own resources?

SOURCES

1. HENRY VIII: FINANCING AN EXTRAVAGANT MONARCH

Source A: from Hall's *Chronicle*. Hall's account of proceedings in Parliament in 1523.

The Parliament being begun, the Cardinal, accompanied with divers Lords, came the 29th day of April into the Common House, where he eloquently declared to the Commons how the King of necessity was driven to war and defence, which in no wise could be maintained without great sums of money, and he thought no less than 800,000 pounds, to be raised of the fifth part of every man's goods and lands, that is to say four shillings of every pound, for he said that the year following the King and the Emperor should make such war in France as hath not been seen.

After long reasoning, there were certain appointed to declare the impossibility of this demand to the Cardinal, which, according to their commission, declared to him substantially the poverty and scarceness of the realm; all which reasons and demonstrations he little regarded, and then the said persons most meekly beseeched his Grace to move the King's Highness to be content with a more easier sum, to which he answered that he would rather have his tongue plucked out of his head than to move the King to take any less sum.

Source B: from Hall's *Chronicle*. Hall's account of popular reaction to the Amicable Grant of 1525.

When this matter was opened through England, how the great men took it was marvel: the poor cursed, the rich repugned [opposed], the light wits railed, but in conclusion all people cursed the Cardinal as subversor of the laws and liberty of England. For, they said, if men should give their goods by a commission, then were it worse than the laws of France, and so England should be bond and not free.

Then the Cardinal wrote letters to all commissioners of the realm that they should keep their first instruction, and in no wise swerve one jot, upon pain of their lives. But for all that could be persuaded, said, lied and flattered, the demand could not be assented to, [people] saying that they that sent forth such commissioners were subverters of the law and worthy to be punished as traitors.

The Duke of Suffolk sat in Suffolk in like commission and by gentle handling caused the rich clothiers to assent and grant the sixth part. They called [their workers] to them and said; Sirs, we be not able to set you to work, our goods be taken from us, and men that had no work began to rage and assemble themselves in companies, and of [several] towns about there rebelled four thousand men, and began to come together still more. The gentlemen that were with the Duke did so much that all the bridges were broken, so that [the rebels'] assembly was somewhat letted. Then the demand for money ceased in all the realm, for well it was perceived that the commons would pay none.

Source C: part of a state paper prepared by Thomas Cromwell in 1534. In it he proposes measures for the seizure of church assets by the crown and the institution of a salaried clergy.

Things to be moved for the King's Highness for an increase and augmentation to be had for maintenance of his most royal estate, and for the defence of the realm, and necessary to be provided for taking away the excess which is the great cause of the abuses of the Church.

1. That it may be provided by Parliament that the Archbishop of Canterbury may have 2,000 marks yearly and not above, and that the residue of the possessions of the Archbishop may be made sure to the King and his heirs for the defence of the realm and maintenance of his royal estate.
2. That the Archbishop of York may have 1,000 pounds yearly for the maintenance of his estate, and the residue to be to the King and his heirs.
3. That the King may have, for the maintenance of the estate of the Supreme Head of the Church of England, the first fruits of every bishopric and benefice for one year after the vacation.
4. That the King may have, for the maintenance of his royal estate, the lands and possessions of all monasteries of which the number is under 13 persons.

Source D: from an Act for the Dissolution of the Abbeys, May 1539.

Where divers and sundry abbots of their own free and voluntary minds, good wills and assents, without constraint, coercion or compulsion of any manner of person or persons, by the due order and course of the common laws of this realm, have severally given and granted all their said monasteries, and all their sites, circuits and precincts of the same, to have and to hold to our sovereign lord the King, his heirs and successors, for ever. Be it therefore enacted by the King our sovereign lord and the lords spiritual and temporal and the Commons in this present parliament assembled, that the King shall have, hold, possess and enjoy for ever all and singular such late monasteries.

Source E: from a letter written by Lord Chancellor Wriothesley to the Privy Council, September 1545.

As to money, I trust you will consider what is done already. This year and last the King has spent about 1,300,000 pounds, his subsidy and benevolence ministering scant 300,000 pounds and the lands consumed and the plate of the realm melted and coined. I lament the danger of the time to come. There is to be repaid in Flanders as much and more than all the rest. Though the King might have a greater grant than the realm could bear, it would do little to the continuance of the charges this winter, most of the subsidy being paid, the revenues received before hand and more borrowed from the mint than will be repaid these four or five months. And yet you write me still, pay, pay, prepare for this and that.

Questions

1. Explain the following references that occur in the sources: 'all commissioners of the realm' (Source B); 'the first fruits of every bishopric' (Source C); 'the plate of the realm melted and coined' (Source E).
2. Compare the opposition met by Wolsey to his financial demands in Source A and in Source B.
3. In what ways would Cromwell's proposals in Source C help to overcome the problems outlined in Sources A and B?
*4. To what extent do these sources suggest that Cromwell tackled the financial problems of Henry VIII more successfully than Wolsey?

Worked answer

*4. [This question proceeds naturally from Question 3. In answering that question the student will already have contrasted the methods employed by Wolsey and by Cromwell to finance the crown and its policies. The student is now required to use the other sources in order to gauge the impact of the respective policies, and their ultimate success in providing Henry with an income adequate for his purposes. Although the question does not specifically require the student to employ background knowledge, such knowledge will provide the student with a framework into which the sources may be fitted.]

As has been established in answering question 3, Wolsey and Cromwell employed significantly different means to raise money for the crown. In Source A Wolsey attempts to raise money for the defence of the realm by seeking a substantial grant of taxation from Parliament. The grant of 1523, like the Amicable Grant of 1525, with which Source B is concerned, is to be raised by a tax assessed as a proportion of the goods of each taxpayer. Sources A and B indicate that such tactics could encounter two problems that undermined their effectiveness. In Source A, the members of the House of Commons protest at the level of Wolsey's demands and try to persuade him to accept a smaller grant. Source B indicates the unrest that might arise from the collection of an unpopular tax. Open rebellion was one of the perennial fears of the Tudor monarchy, and Henry VIII was always more likely to abandon demands for taxation rather than risk such instability. The combined impression of these sources alone is that Wolsey was unsuccessful in meeting the financial demands of Henry's policies in the mid-1520s.

In Source C Cromwell pursues a very different policy. He concentrates upon the property and income of the Church rather that those of wealthy laymen. His proposal is to raise money by paying salaries to leading churchmen, and diverting the substantial residue of Church property into the coffers of the crown. Cromwell does not simply aim to meet a current emergency, but states that his aim is to achieve 'an increase and augmentation of [Henry's] most royal estate', to provide the King with sources of landed and other income which will enrich the monarchy in the long term. Yet Source C is only a 'state paper', an abstract proposal, and it was never implemented in full. Source D, on the other hand, illustrates that the crown did indeed seize the property of the monasteries.

This comparison of projects and consequences tends to show Cromwell in a better light than Wolsey. Source E, however, suggests that Cromwell's project did not, in fact, achieve its long-term aim of providing the crown with an adequate income. Wriothesley details the sums spent by Henry in 1544–45, and outlines some of the measures that the crown has had to take. In particular, he mentions 'the lands consumed': a reference to the sale of some of those very monastic lands with which Cromwell endowed the crown. Wriothesley's reference to 'a greater grant than the realm could bear' seems to take Henrician finances back to the parliamentary tensions of Source A, and might lead to the conclusion that, in the long run, Cromwell's success had been no greater than Wolsey's.

SOURCES

2. TRYING TO BALANCE THE BOOKS IN THE REIGN OF ELIZABETH

Source F: from Sir Thomas Gresham's advice to Elizabeth on the fall of exchanges, 1558.

It may please your Majesty to understand that the first occasion of the fall of the exchange did grow by the King's Majesty, your late father, in abasing his coins from vi ounces fine to iii ounces fine. Whereupon the exchange fell from xxvi s [shillings] viii d [pence] to xiii s iv d which was the occasion that all your fine gold was conveyed out of this your realm.

Secondly, by reason of his wars, the King's Majesty fell into great debts in Flanders. And for the payment thereof they had no other device but to pay it by exchange, and to carry over his fine gold for the payment of the same.

As the exchange is the thing that eats out all princes, if it be not substantially looked into, so likewise the exchange is the chiefest and richest thing only above all other, to restore your Majesty and your realm to fine gold and silver, and is the mean that makes all foreign commodities and your own commodities with all kind of victual [foodstuffs] good cheap, and likewise keeps your fine gold and silver within your realm. Your Highness hath no other ways, but when time and opportunity serveth, to bring your base money into fine of xi ounces fine, and so gold after the rate.

Source G: part of a speech made by Sir Walter Mildmay to the House of Commons, 1576.

Her Majesty hath most carefully delivered this Kingdom from a great and weighty debt, wherewith it hath long been burdened. A debt began four years at the least before the death of King Henry the Eighth, and not cleared until within these two years, and all that while running upon interest, a course able to eat up not only private men and their patrimonies, but also princes and their estates. But such hath been the care of this time, as her Majesty and the State is clearly freed from the eating corrosive, the truth whereof may be testified by the citizens of London, whose bonds under the common seal of the city of assurance of payment are now all discharged, cancelled and delivered. By means whereof the realm is not only acquitted of this great burden, and the merchants free, but also her Majesty's credit both at home and abroad greater than any other prince for money, if she need have.

Source H: from the minutes of the parliamentary deliberations over taxation, 1593.

Sir Robert Cecil showed unto the committees of this House the great and present need of provision of treasure to be employed for the defence of the realm against the invasion of the great and mighty enemies unto this realm and state; and showing further, that the double subsidy and Fifteenths and Tenths lastly granted unto her Majesty, amounting but unto two hundred and four score thousand pounds, her Majesty has nevertheless in these defensive wars expended of her own treasure alone ten hundred and thirty thousand pounds since the time of the granting of the said double subsidy.

Sergeant Harris moved for three subsidies, but the ancient custom of payment to be retained.

Sir John Fortescue thought it liberal to grant three subsidies, but did assure of his proper knowledge that three subsidies would not defray her Majesty's charges.

Mr Heale argued the wealth of the country to be greater than ever it was, affirming that the country was richer many thousands of pounds than heretofore. He thought more subsidies would be yielded.

Mr Francis Bacon assented to three subsidies, and to this propounded three questions. The first, impossibility or difficulty; the second, danger of discontentment; and thirdly, a better manner of supply than subsidy. For impossibility: the poor men's rent is such that they are not able to yield it, nor to pay so much for the present. The gentlemen must sell their plate, and the farmers their brass pots, ere this will be paid. And for us we are here to search the wounds of the realm and not to skin them over: therefore not to persuade ourselves of their wealth more than it is. The dangers are these. We shall first breed discontentment in paying these subsidies, and in the cause endanger her Majesty's safety, which must consist more in the love of the people than in their wealth; and therefore not to give them discontentment in paying these subsidies.

Source I: from a letter from the Council to Commissioners for the parliamentary subsidy, 26 July 1598.

And yet these subsidies of later times have come to far less sums than those of former ages; which cannot grow but by the remiss and neglectful dealing of such as are Commissioners for the assessment of the same. You cannot perform the trust reposed in you, nor your duties towards her Majesty and your country, if you proceed not in this service with great care and endeavour to advance the sums and assessments as much as may be, assessing all men indifferently that are of ability, without regard to any favour. For it hath been noted heretofore that this burden is laid upon the meaner sort who are less able indeed to bear the burden; and the wealthier and best able to spare the same are too favourably dealt withal, the Commissioners bearing one with another, and every of them bearing with their own private friends and followers.

Source J: summary of the government's income and expenditure in 1600, from the *Calendar of State papers Domestic, Elizabeth*.

Income		Expenditure	
Income from justice	10,000	Privy Purse	2,000
Income from crown lands	60,000	Wardrobe	4,000
Sale of crown lands	4,000	Household	4,000
Customs and excise	80,000	Officer of the works	5,000
Wine duties	24,000	Various naval costs	23,000
Recusancy fines	7,000	Campaigns in	
First Fruits and Tenths	20,000	Ireland	320,000
Subsidy of Clergy	20,000	Low Countries	25,000
Subsidy of laity	80,000	Fees and annuities	26,000
15ths and 10ths	60,000	[plus a number of smaller sums]	
[plus a number of smaller sums]			
Total	374,000	Total	459,840

Questions

1. Explain the following references that occur in the sources: 'abasing his coins' (Source F); 'in these defensive wars' (Source H); 'bearing with their own private friends' (Source I).
2. Summarise in your own words the arguments put forward in Sources F and G about the major financial problems facing the government at the beginning of Elizabeth's reign.
3. Compare and contrast the arguments put forward in Sources G and H for the granting of taxation by Parliament.
*4. What evidence is there in Sources H and I to suggest that parliamentary taxation was not always a satisfactory answer to the government's financial needs?
5. 'In Elizabeth's reign, government finances were adequate for peacetime purposes, but could not cope with the costs of war.' To what extent do these sources lead you to agree with this statement?

Worked answer

*4. [The question requires the student to understand the arguments put forward in the two sources, often couched in relatively unfamiliar language, and then to set those arguments in the context of the student's background knowledge. In this case it is necessary to understand the crown's financial needs in the 1590s, together with the social and economic problems of the decade.]

Sources H and I are both concerned with the raising of parliamentary taxation, although they deal with different stages in the process. Source H illustrates the arguments to which taxation was subject in Parliament. Sir John Fortescue asserts that the proposed grant of three subsidies was too small to meet the crown's needs. Beyond that it might be noted that some members oppose taxation, as Francis Bacon does, and indeed that Bacon puts forward some convincing arguments. He not only claims that many taxpayers will be hard pressed to pay the proposed taxes, but adds that such financial demands may lead to discontent and rebellion. Background knowledge of the period indicates that the mid-1590s were indeed years of great economic hardship and some discontent.

Source I turns to the processes by which such parliamentary grants were actually collected. The Council protests to the commissioners responsible for the assessment and collection of the subsidies in the localities that the grant is not producing the expected sums. This is ascribed to malpractice on the part of the local commissioners, who are liable to under-assess themselves, and to serve their own local political interests by performing a similar favour for their friends and clients.

NOTES AND SOURCES

1. THE PERSONAL ELEMENT IN TUDOR MONARCHY

1 J.R. Green. *Short History of the English People*. London. 1874.
2 F.C. Dietz. *English Public Finance 1485–1641*. London. 1964.
3 K.W. Pickthorn. *Early Tudor Government*. Cambridge. 1934.
4 G.R. Elton. *The Tudor Constitution*. Cambridge. 1960.
5 Attainder: an act of Parliament declaring an individual to be guilty of treason. Such an act automatically involved the forfeiture to the crown of the property and titles of that individual.
6 Bonds and recognisances: legal documents between the king and a subject whereby the latter acknowledged his responsibility, either for his own good behaviour or for that of another individual. Failure to fulfil the guarantee of good behaviour involved the forfeiture of a specified sum of money.
7 J.R. Lander. *Crown and Nobility, 1450–1509*. London. 1976; and *Government and Community. England 1450–1509*. London. 1980.
8 R. Lockyer. *Henry VII*. London and New York. 1968.
9 G.R. Elton. 'Henry VII: Rapacity and Remorse'. In Elton, *Studies in Tudor and Stuart Politics and Government*. Cambridge. 1974.
10 J.A.F. Thomson. *The Transformation of Medieval England, 1370–1529*. London and New York. 1983.
11 S.B. Chrimes. *Henry VII*. London. 1972.
12 C. Carpenter. 'Henry VII and the English Polity'. In B. Thompson (ed.), *The Reign of Henry VII*. Stamford. 1995.
13 M. Condon. 'Ruling Elites in the Reign of Henry VII'. In J. Guy (ed.), *The Tudor Monarchy*. London. 1997.
14 B. Thompson. 'The Place of Henry VII in English History'. In B. Thompson (ed.), *The Reign of Henry VII*. Stamford. 1995.
15 Edward Seymour was made Earl of Hertford in 1537, and did not acquire the title of Duke of Somerset until 1547, a few days after

taking office as Lord Protector. Similarly, John Dudley was successively Viscount Lisle (1542) and Earl of Warwick (1546), only assuming the dignity of Duke of Northumberland in October 1551. For the sake of simplicity, however, they are referred to throughout by their ultimate titles.

16 D.E. Hoak. *The King's Council in the Reign of Edward VI*. Cambridge. 1976; and 'Rehabilitating the Duke of Northumberland'. In J. Loach and R. Tittler (eds), *The Mid-Tudor Polity c. 1540–1560*. London. 1980.

17 W.G. Hoskins. *The Age of Plunder: The England of Henry VIII 1500–1547*. London. 1976.

18 A.F. Pollard. *England under Protector Somerset*. London. 1900.

19 M. Bush. *The Government Policy of Protector Somerset*. London. 1975.

20 J. Murphy. 'The Illusion of Decline: The Privy Chamber 1547–1558'. In D. Starkey (ed.), *The English Court from the Wars of the Roses to the Civil War*. London and New York. 1987.

21 D. Loades. *Essays in the Reign of Edward VI*. Bangor. 1994; and *John Dudley, Duke of Northumberland, 1504–1553*. Oxford. 1996.

22 W.K. Jordan. *Edward VI: The Young King. The Protectorship of the Duke of Somerset*. London. 1968; and *Edward VI: The Threshold of Power; the Dominance of the Duke of Northumberland*. London. 1970.

23 P. Williams. *The Later Tudors, England 1547–1603*. Oxford. 1995.

24 B.L. Beer. *Northumberland. The Political Career of John Dudley, Earl of Warwick and Duke of Northumberland*. Kent, OH. 1973.

Source A: D. Hay (ed.). *The Anglica Historia 1485–1537*. London. 1950.

Source B: F. Bacon. *History of the Reign of Henry VII*. London. 1971. p. 229.

Source C: R. Lockyer. *Henry VII*. London. 1983. p. 86.

Source D: I. Arthurson. *Documents of the Reign of Henry VII*. Cambridge. 1984. p. 106.

Source E: C.H. Williams (ed.). *English Historical Documents 1485–1558*. London. 1967.

Source F: P.W. Chambers. *Thomas More*. London. 1935. pp. 99–100.

Source G: M. Levine. *Tudor Dynastic Problems, 1450–1571*. London. 1973. p. 163.

Source H: Ibid. p. 167.

Source I: S. Newman. *Reading Historical Documents. Yorkists and Tudors*. Oxford. 1989. p. 35.

Source J: Ibid. p. 34.

Source K: R. Tittler. *The Reign of Mary I*. London. 1983. pp. 85–86.

Source L: M. Levine. *Tudor Dynastic Problems, 1450–1571*. London. 1973. p. 171.

2. COURT AND PATRONAGE

1 D. Loades. *Tudor Government*. Oxford. 1997. p. 249.
2 R. O'Day. 'Ecclesiastical Patronage: Who Controlled the Church?' In F. Heal and R. O'Day (eds), *Church and Society in England: Henry VIII to James I*. London. 1977. p. 137.
3 A.F. Pollard. *Henry VIII*. London. 1902; and *Wolsey*. London. 1929.
4 The phrase is not Pollard's, but is coined to encapsulate Pollard's view by John Kenyon in *The History Men. The Historical Profession in England since the Renaissance*. London. 1983.
5 G.R. Elton. *Henry VIII: An Essay in Revision*. London. 1962.
6 George Cavendish served Wolsey as gentleman usher during his last years in power. The most recent edition of his biography of his master, *The Life of Cardinal Wolsey*, probably written between 1554 and 1557, was published in 1959.
7 Polydore Vergil was an Italian humanist who arrived in England as a papal official (1501) and became an English subject in 1510. Consistently hostile to Wolsey, he was imprisoned for slandering the Cardinal in 1515. His history of the early Tudor years, *Anglica Historia*, was published in Basle in 1534.
8 P. Gwyn. *The King's Cardinal. The Rise and Fall of Thomas Wolsey*. London. 1990.
9 D. Starkey. 'Intimacy and Innovation: The Rise of the Privy Chamber 1485–1547'. In D. Starkey (ed.), *The English Court from the Wars of the Roses to the Civil War*. London and New York. 1987; and *The Reign of Henry VIII. Personalities and Politics*, London. 1985.
10 J. Guy. 'Wolsey, Cromwell and the Reform of Government'. In D. MacCulloch (ed.), *The Reign of Henry VIII. Politics, Policy and Piety*. London. 1995.
11 J.J. Scarisbrick. *Henry VIII*. London. 1968.
12 P. Wright. 'A Change in Direction: The Ramifications of a Female Household'. In D. Starkey (ed.), *The English Court from the Wars of the Roses to the Civil War*. London and New York. 1987.
13 C. Haigh. *Elizabeth I*. London and New York. 1988.
14 William Cecil was only created Lord Burghley in 1571. His younger son, Robert Cecil, rose steadily in the royal service, becoming the Queen's Principal Secretary in 1596, and succeeding his father as the crown's chief minister upon

Burghley's death in 1598. To avoid confusion between the two, I've generally referred to the father as 'Burghley' and to the son as 'Cecil'.

15 S. Adams. 'Favourites and Factions at the Elizabethan Court'. In J. Guy (ed.), *The Tudor Monarchy*. London. 1997; and 'Eliza Enthroned? The Court and its Politics'. In C. Haigh (ed.), *The Reign of Elizabeth I*. London. 1984.

16 J.E. Neale. 'The Elizabethan Political Scene'. In J. E. Neale, *Essays in Elizabethan History*. London. 1958.

17 W. MacCaffrey. *The Shaping of the Elizabethan Regime*. London. 1969.

18 'Courtly love' was a prominent concept in the secular literature of late medieval Europe. By its conventions the noble lady was the object of desire of knights and heroes, who dedicated their acts of valour to her. Its strong, yet unconsummated, sexual element made the woman at once an object of desire and of respect.

19 P. Williams. *The Later Tudors. England 1547–1603*. Oxford. 1995.

20 'Gloriana' was one of a variety of names by which poets and composers of masques and pageants referred to Elizabeth. Others, such as 'Belphoebe' (an alternative name for the goddess Diana) and 'Astraea' (the daughter of Zeus, and goddess of justice), linked her to classical mythology.

21 J. Guy. *The Reign of Elizabeth I: Court and Culture in the Last Decade*. Cambridge. 1995.

Source A: G. Cavendish. *The Life of Cardinal Wolsey*. London. 1890. pp. 24–25.

Source B: D. Starkey. *The Reign of Henry VIII. Personalities and Politics*. London. 1985. p. 61.

Source C: A.F. Pollard. *Wolsey*. London. 1965. p. 101.

Source D: C.H. Williams (ed.). *English Historical Documents 1485–1558*. London. 1967.

Source E: J.J. Scarisbrick. *Henry VIII*. London. 1968. Illustration facing p. 82.

Source F: G. Cavendish. *The Life of Cardinal Wolsey*. London. 1890. pp. 250–51.

Source G: L. Baldwin Smith. *Elizabeth I*. St Louis, MO. pp. 24–25.

Source H: Ibid. pp. 62–63.

Source I: S. Newman. *Reading Historical Documents. Yorkists and Tudors*. Oxford. 1989. p. 61.

Source J: D. O'Sullivan and R. Lockyer. *Longman Sources and Opinions. Tudor England*. London. 1993. p. 59.

Source K: J.E. Neale. *Essays in Elizabethan History*. London. 1958. pp. 38–39.

3. THE CENTRAL ORGANS AND OFFICES OF GOVERNMENT

1 Elton quoted by C. Coleman. 'Professor Elton's "Revolution"'. In C. Coleman and D. Starkey (eds), *Revolution Reassessed. Revisions in the History of Tudor Government and Administration.* Oxford. 1986. p. 8.

2 G.R. Elton. *The Tudor Revolution in Government.* Cambridge. 1953; *The Tudor Constitution.* Cambridge. 1960; *Reform and Reformation. England 1509–1558.* London. 1977.

3 J. Guy. 'Privy Council: Revolution or Evolution?' In C. Coleman and D. Starkey (eds), *Revolution Reassessed. Revisions in the History of Tudor Government and Administration.* Oxford. 1986; 'Wolsey, Cromwell and the Reform of Government'. In D. MacCulloch (ed.), *The Reign of Henry VIII. Politics, Policy and Piety.* London. 1995.

4 D. Starkey. *The Reign of Henry VIII: Personalities and Politics.* London. 1985; 'Which Age of Reform?' and 'After the Revolution'. Both in C. Coleman and D. Starkey (eds), *Revolution Reassessed. Revisions in the History of Tudor Government and Administration.* Oxford. 1986.

5 D. Loades. *Tudor Government. Structures of Authority in the Sixteenth Century.* Oxford. 1997.

6 C. Coleman. 'Professor Elton's "Revolution"'. In C. Coleman and D. Starkey (eds), *Revolution Reassessed. Revisions in the History of Tudor Government and Administration.* Oxford. 1986.

7 J.D. Alsop. *The Structure of Early Tudor Finance.* In C. Coleman and D. Starkey (eds), *Revolution Reassessed. Revisions in the History of Tudor Government and Administration.* Oxford. 1986.

8 A.F. Pollard. *A History of England from the Accession of Edward VI to the Death of Elizabeth.* London. 1910.

9 D. Hoak. 'Two Revolutions in Tudor Government: The Formation and Organisation of Mary I's Privy Council'. In C. Coleman and D. Starkey (eds) *Revolution Reassessed. Revisions in the History of Tudor Government and Administration.* Oxford. 1986.

10 A. Weikel. 'The Marian Council Revisited'. In J. Loach and R. Tittler (eds), *The Mid-Tudor Polity. c.1540–1560.* London. 1980.

11 D. Loades. *The Reign of Mary Tudor: Politics, Government and Religion in England, 1553–58.* London. 1979; *Mary Tudor. A Life.* Oxford. 1989.

12 P. Donaldson. *A Machiavellian Treatise by Stephen Gardiner.* London. 1975.

13 G.R. Elton. *The Tudor Constitution.* Cambridge. 1960.

Source A: C.H. Williams (ed.). *English Historical Documents 1485–1558.* London. 1967.

Source B: J.R. Tanner. *Tudor Constitutional Documents*. Cambridge. 1951. p. 211.

Source C: S. Newman. *Reading Historical Documents. Yorkists and Tudors 1450–1603*. Oxford. p. 59.

Source D: J. Youings. *The Dissolution of the Monasteries*. London. 1971. p. 229.

Source E: J.R. Tanner. *Tudor Constitutional Documents*. Cambridge. 1951. pp. 206–07.

Source F: J.A. Froude. *The Reign of Mary Tudor*. London. 1910. p. 21n.

Source G: Ibid. p. 241n.

Source H: M.A.R. Graves. *Early Tudor Parliaments 1485–1558*. London. 1990. pp. 101–02.

Source I: J.R. Tanner. *Tudor Constitutional Documents*. Cambridge. 1951. p. 224.

4. CENTRAL GOVERNMENT: LAW AND ORDER

1 F. Metzger. 'The Last Phase of the Medieval Chancery'. In A. Harding (ed.), *Law-making and Law-makers in British History*. London. 1980.

2 J. Guy. *The Cardinal's Court*. Brighton. 1977; *Tudor England*. Oxford. 1988.

3 A.F. Pollard. *Wolsey*. London. 1929.

4 G.R. Elton. 'Introduction' to the 1965 edition of Pollard's *Wolsey*.

5 P. Gwyn. *The King's Cardinal: The Rise and Fall of Thomas Wolsey*. London. 1990.

6 D. MacCulloch. 'The Consolidation of England'. In J. Morrill (ed.), *The Oxford Illustrated History of Tudor and Stuart Britain*. Oxford. 1996.

7 J.J. Scarisbrick. 'Cardinal Wolsey and the Common Weal'. In *Wealth and Power in Tudor England. Essays presented to S.T. Bindoff*. London. 1978.

8 C. Brooks. 'A Law-abiding and Litigious Society'. In J. Morrill (ed.), *The Oxford Illustrated History of Tudor and Stuart Britain*. Oxford. 1996.

9 J. Youings. *The Pelican Social History of Britain. Sixteenth Century England*. Harmondsworth. 1984.

10 L. Stone. *The Crisis of the Aristocracy 1588–1641*. Oxford. 1965.

11 P. Williams. *The Tudor Regime*. Oxford. 1979.

12 J.S. Cockburn. *Crime in England 1550–1800*. London. 1977.

13 A.L. Beier. 'Social Problems in Elizabethan London'. In J. Barry (ed.), *The Tudor and Stuart Town 1530–1688*. London and New York. 1990.

14 J. Pound. *Poverty and Vagrancy in Tudor England*. London. 1971.

15 P. Clark. *English Provincial Society from the Reformation to the Revolution: Religion, Politics and Society in Kent 1500–1640.* Hassocks. 1977.

16 A.G.R. Smith. *The Emergence of a Nation State: The Commonwealth of England 1529–1660*. London and New York. 1984.

17 K. Wrightson. *English Society 1580–1680*. London. 1982.

18 D.M. Palliser. *The Age of Elizabeth. England under the Later Tudors 1547–1603*. London and New York. 1983.

Source A: Wibley (ed.). *Hall's Chronicle*. London. 1904. p.15.

Source B: S.J. Gunn and P.G. Lindley (eds). *Cardinal Wolsey. Church, State and Art*. Cambridge. 1991. p. 54.

Source C: M.D. Palmer. *Henry VIII*. London. 1983. pp. 91–92.

Source D: P. Gwyn. *The King's Cardinal. The Rise and Fall of Thomas Wolsey*. London. 1990. p. 420.

Source E: C.H. Williams (ed.). *English Historical Documents 1485–1558*. London. 1967.

Source F: D. Hay (ed.). *The Anglica Historia 1485–1537*. London. 1950.

Source G: G.W. Prothero. *Statutes and Constitutional Documents, 1558–1625*. Oxford. 1913. p. 179.

Source H: Conyers Read. *William Lambarde and Local Government*. New York. 1962. pp. 182–84.

Source I: J. Pound. *Poverty and Vagrancy in Tudor England*. London. 1986. pp. 87–90.

Source J: D. O'Sullivan and R. Lockyer. *Longman Sources and Opinions. Tudor England*. London. 1993. pp. 77–78.

5. THE GOVERNMENT OF THE LOCALITIES

1 S. Ellis. *Tudor Frontiers and Noble Power. The Making of the British State*. Oxford. 1995; and *Tudor Ireland. Crown, Community and the Conflict of Cultures, 1470–1603*. London and New York. 1985.

2 The Fitzgerald family had held this title for eight generations before the accession of the Tudors. The period under consideration was dominated by the 8th Earl (1478–1513) and the 9th Earl of Kildare (1513–34), both named Gerald.

3 E. Curtis. *A History of Medieval Ireland from 1086 to 1513*. London. 1938.

4 S. Chrimes. *Henry VII*. London. 1972.

5 D. Loades. *Tudor Government*. Oxford. 1997.

6 See, for instance, J.F. Lydon. *Ireland in the Later Middle Ages*. Dublin. 1972; *The English in Medieval Ireland*. Dublin. 1984.

7 G.R. Elton. *Reform and Reformation. England 1509–1558*. London. 1977.
8 G. Morton. *Elizabethan Ireland*. London and New York. 1971.
9 R.D. Edwards. *Church and State in Tudor Ireland*. Dublin. 1935.
10 F.J. Fisher. 'Commercial Trends and Policy in Sixteenth Century England'. In *Economic History Review*. 1939–40.
11 P. Ramsey. *Tudor Economic Problems*. London. 1963.
12 J. Pound. *Poverty and Vagrancy in Tudor England*. London and New York. 1971.
13 J. Neale. *Elizabeth I and her Parliaments*. London. 1953–57.
14 S.T. Bindoff. 'The Making of the Statute of Artificers'. In *Elizabethan Government and Society*. London. 1961.
15 W.K. Jordan. *Philanthropy in England, 1480–1660*. London. 1959.
16 P. Slack. 'Poverty and Social Regulation in Elizabethan England'. In C. Haigh (ed.), *The Reign of Elizabeth I*. London. 1984; and *The Impact of Plague in Tudor and Stuart England*. London. 1985.
17 M.G. Davies. *The Enforcement of English Apprenticeship, 1563–1642*. Cambridge, MA. 1956.
18 B. Coward. *Social Change and Continuity in Early Modern England, 1550–1750*. London and New York. 1988.
Source A: A.F. Pollard. *The Reign of Henry VII from Contemporary Sources. Vol. III*. London. 1914. pp. 259–60.
Source B: Ibid. p. 265.
Source C: Ibid. pp. 269–70.
Source D: Ibid. p. 272.
Source E: Ibid. p. 285.
Source F: Ibid. pp. 290–91.
Source G: G.W. Prothero. *Statutes and Constitutional Documents, 1558–1625*. Oxford. 1913. pp. 39–45.
Source H: Ibid. pp. 67–72.
Source I: Ibid. pp. 72–74.
Source J: Ibid. pp. 103–05.
Source K: J. Pound. *Poverty and Vagrancy in Tudor England*. London. 1986. p. 87.

6. THE ROLE OF PARLIAMENT

1 S.B. Chrimes. *Henry VII*. London. 1972.
2 M.A.R. Graves. *The Tudor Parliaments. Crown, Lords and Commons, 1485–1603*. London and New York. 1985; *Early Tudor Parliaments, 1485–1558*. London and New York. 1990.
3 G.W. Bernard. *War, Taxation and Rebellion in Tudor England*. Brighton. 1986.

4 D. Loades. *Tudor Government. Structures of Authority in the Sixteenth Century*. Oxford. 1997.

5 S.E. Lehmberg. *The Reformation Parliament, 1529–1536*. Cambridge. 1970; *The Later Parliaments of Henry VIII, 1536–1547*. Cambridge. 1977.

6 J.E. Neale. *The Elizabethan House of Commons*. London. 1949; *Elizabeth I and her Parliaments*. Two volumes. London. 1953.

7 W. Notestein. *The Winning of the Initiative by the House of Commons*. London. 1924/25; *The House of Commons, 1604–1610*. New Haven. 1971.

8 N. Jones. *Faith by Statute. Parliament and the Settlement of Religion, 1559*. London. 1982.

9 G.R. Elton. 'Tudor Government: Points of Contact: The Parliament'. In *Studies in Tudor and Stuart Government and Politics*. Cambridge. 1983; 'Parliament'. In C. Haigh (ed.), *The Reign of Elizabeth I*. London. 1984; *The Parliament of England, 1559–81*. Cambridge. 1986.

10 M.A.R. Graves. *The Tudor Parliaments. Crown, Lords and Commons, 1485–1603*. London and New York. 1985; *Elizabethan Parliaments, 1559–1601*. London and New York. 1987.

11 D. Loades. *Tudor Government, Structures of Authority in the Sixteenth Century*. Oxford. 1997.

12 J. Guy. *Tudor England*. Oxford. 1988.

13 J. Loach. *Parliament under the Tudors*. Oxford. 1991.

Source A: M.A.R. Graves. *Early Tudor Parliaments 1485–1558*. London. 1990. p. 83.

Source B: Ibid. p. 84.

Source C: M. Bateson. 'Letters and Papers of Henry VIII'. In *English Historical Review*. 1890. pp. 550–73.

Source D: M. Levine. *Tudor Dynastic Problems*. London. 1973. pp. 172–73.

Source E: J. Hurstfield and A.G.R. Smith. *Elizabethan People: State and Society*. London. 1977. p. 149.

Source F: T.E. Hartley (ed.). *Proceedings in the Parliaments of Elizabeth I. Vol. I. 1558–1581*. Leicester. 1981. pp. 33–39.

Source G: G.W. Prothero. *Statutes and Constitutional Documents, 1558–1625*. Oxford. 1913. p. 124.

Source H: T.E. Hartley (ed.). *Proceedings in the Parliaments of Elizabeth I. Vol. I. 1558–1581*. Leicester. 1981. p. 154.

Source I: M.A.R. Graves. *Elizabethan Parliaments 1559–1601*. London. 1987. p. 103.

Source J: Ibid. pp. 95–96.

7. GOVERNMENT OF THE CHURCH

1   J.J. Scarisbrick. *The Reformation and the English People*. Oxford. 1984.
2   E. Duffy. *The Stripping of the Altars. Traditional Religion in England, 1400–1580*. New Haven and London. 1992.
3   J. Guy. *Tudor England*. Oxford. 1988.
4   A. Fox and J. Guy. *Reassessing the Henrician Age: Humanism, Politics and Reform, 1500–1550*. Oxford 1986.
5   S.B. Chrimes. *Henry VII*. London. 1972.
6   C. Haigh. *English Reformations. Religion, Politics and Society under the Tudors*. Oxford. 1993.
7   J.A.F. Thomson. *The Transformation of Medieval England, 1370–1529*, London and New York. 1983; *The Early Tudor Church and Society, 1485–1529*. London and New York. 1993.
8   W.E. Lunt. *Financial Relations of the Papacy with England, 1327–1534*. Cambridge, MA. 1962.
9   A.G. Dickens. *The English Reformation*. London. 1964.
10 A.F. Pollard. *Wolsey*. London. 1929.
11 P. Gwyn. *The King's Cardinal. The Rise and Fall of Thomas Wolsey*. London. 1990.
12 C. Harper-Bill. *The Pre-Reformation Church in England, 1400–1530*. London and New York. 1989.
13 G.R. Elton. *The Tudor Revolution in Government*. Cambridge. 1953.
14 C. Haigh. 'The Continuity of Catholicism in the English Reformation'. In C. Haigh (ed.), *The English Reformation Revised*. Cambridge. 1987; *English Reformations. Religion, Politics and Society under the Tudors*. Oxford. 1993.
15 R. Hutton. 'The Local Impact of the Tudor Reformations'. In P. Marshall (ed.), *The Impact of the English Reformation, 1500–1640*. London and New York. 1997.
16 A.G. Dickens. 'The First Stages of Romanist Recusancy in Yorkshire, 1560–1590'. In *Reformation Studies*. London. 1982.
17 Recusancy: refusal to attend the services of the established Church.
18 J.J. Scarisbrick. *The Reformation and the English People*. Oxford. 1984.
19 D.M. Palliser. 'Popular Reactions to the Reformation during the Years of Uncertainty, 1530–70'. In F. Heal and R. O'Day (eds), *Church and Society in England: Henry VIII to James I*. London. 1977.
20 Visitation: the process by which bishops inspected the state of religious practice within their dioceses.
21 J.E. Neale. *Elizabeth I and her Parliaments*. London. 1953–57.

22 R. Houlbrooke. 'The Protestant Episcopate 1547–1603: The Pastoral Contribution'. In F. Heal and R. O'Day (eds), *Church and Society in England: Henry VIII to James I*. London. 1977.

23 R. O'Day. 'Ecclesiastical Patronage: Who Controlled the Church?' In F. Heal and R. O'Day (eds), *Church and Society in England: Henry VIII to James I*. London. 1977.

24 C. Cross. *The Royal Supremacy in the Elizabethan Church*. London. 1969; 'Churchmen and the Royal Supremacy'. In F. Heal and R. O'Day (eds), *Church and Society in England: Henry VIII to James I*. London. 1977.

25 P. Collinson. *The Elizabethan Puritan Movement*. London. 1967.

Source A: M. Levine. *Tudor Dynastic Problems*. London. 1973. p. 141.

Source B: I. Arthurson. *Documents of the Reign of Henry VII*. Cambridge. 1984. p. 39.

Source C: A.F. Pollard. *The Reign of Henry VII from Contemporary Sources. Vol. III*. London. 1914. pp. 173–77.

Source D: C. Harper-Bill. *The Pre-Reformation Church in England*. London. 1996. p. 98.

Source E: P. Gwyn. *The King's Cardinal. The Rise and Fall of Thomas Wolsey*. London. 1990. pp. 49–50.

Source F: C. Harper-Bill. *The Pre-Reformation Church in England*. London. 1996. pp. 98–99.

Source G: G.R. Elton. *The Tudor Constitution*. Cambridge. 1965. p. 344.

Source H: C. Cross. *The Royal Supremacy in the Elizabethan Church*. London. 1969. pp. 131–35.

Source I: Sir C. Sharp. *Memorials of the Rebellion of the Earls of Northumberland and Westmorland*. 1840. p. 256.

Source J: G. Regan. *Elizabeth I*. Cambridge. 1988. p. 76.

Source K: D. O'Sullivan and R. Lockyer. *Longman Sources and Opinions. Tudor England*. London. 1993. pp. 11–12.

Source L: C. Cross. *The Royal Supremacy in the Elizabethan Church*. London. 1969. p. 101.

Source M: J. Hurstfield and A.G.R. Smith. *Elizabethan People: State and Society*. London. 1977. pp. 125–27.

Source N: D. O'Sullivan and R. Lockyer. *Longman Sources and Opinions. Tudor England*. London. 1993. p. 36.

8. FINANCE

1 F.C. Dietz. *English Public Finance 1485–1641*. Volume 1. *English Government Finance 1485–1558*. London. 1964.

2 P. Gwyn. *The King's Cardinal. The Rise and Fall of Thomas Wolsey*. London. 1990.

3 J. Guy. 'Wolsey, Cromwell and the Reform of Government'. In D. MacCulloch (ed.), *The Reign of Henry VIII. Politics, Policy and Piety*. London. 1995.

4 R. Hoyle. 'War and Public Finance'. In D. MacCulloch (ed.), *The Reign of Henry VIII. Politics, Policy and Piety*. London. 1995.

5 D. Starkey. *The Reign of Henry VIII. Personalities and Politics*. London. 1985.

6 C.E. Challis. 'The Debasement of the Coinage, 1542–51'. In *Economic History Review*. 1967.

7 D.M. Palliser. *The Age of Elizabeth. England under the Later Tudors, 1547–1603*. London and New York. 1983.

8 A.G.R. Smith. *The Government of Elizabethan England*. London. 1967; *The Emergence of a Nation State. The Commonwealth of England 1529–1660*. London. 1984.

9 C. Read. *Lord Burghley and Queen Elizabeth*. London. 1960.

10 J.D. Alsop. 'Government, Finance and the Community of the Exchequer'. In C. Haigh (ed.), *The Reign of Elizabeth I*. London. 1984.

11 C. Russell. *The Crisis of Parliaments. English History 1509–1630*. Oxford. 1971.

12 L. Stone. *The Crisis of the Aristocracy, 1558–1641*. Oxford. 1965.

13 C. Haigh. 'Politics in an Age of Peace and War, 1570–1630'. In J. Morrill (ed.), *The Oxford Illustrated History of Tudor and Stuart Britain*. Oxford. 1996.

Source A: M.A.R. Graves. *Early Tudor Parliaments 1485–1558*. London. 1990. p.105.

Source B: Ibid. pp. 36–37.

Source C: M.D. Palmer. *Henry VIII*. London. 1983. pp. 104–05.

Source D: J.R. Tanner. *Tudor Constitutional Documents 1485–1603*. Cambridge. 1951. pp. 64–66.

Source E: R. Hoyle. 'War and Public Finance'. In D. MacCulloch (ed.), *The Reign of Henry VIII. Politics, Policy and Piety*. London. 1995. p. 92.

Source F: S. Newman. *Reading Historical Documents*. Yorkists and Tudors. Oxford. 1989. pp. 105–06.

Source G: G. Regan. *Elizabeth I*. Cambridge. 1988. pp. 106–07.

Source H: Ibid. pp. 109–10.

Source I: D. O'Sullivan and R. Lockyer. *Longman Sources and Opinions. Tudor England*. London. 1993. pp. 90–91.

Source J: G. Regan. *Elizabeth I*. Cambridge. 1988. p. 112.

SELECT BIBLIOGRAPHY

The best general works on the Tudor period are probably: J. Guy: *Tudor England* (Oxford 1988); P. Williams: *The Later Tudors, England 1547–1603* (Oxford 1995). For more detailed accounts of specific reigns and periods the student might consult: S.B. Chrimes: *Henry VII* (London 1972); R. Lockyer: *Henry VII* (London 1983); B. Thomson (ed.): *The Reign of Henry VII* (Stamford 1995); J.R. Lander: *Government and Community. England 1450–1509* (London 1980); J.J. Scarisbrick: *Henry VIII* (London 1968); D. Starkey: *The Reign of Henry VIII. Personalities and Politics* (London 1985); M.D. Palmer: *Henry VIII* (London and New York 1983); P. Gwyn: *The King's Cardinal. The Rise and Fall of Thomas Wolsey* (London 1990); D. MacCulloch (ed.): *The Reign of Henry VIII. Politics, Policy and Piety* (London 1995); M. Bush: *The Government Policy of Protector Somerset* (London 1975); D. Loades: *Essays in the Reign of Edward VI* (Bangor 1994); D. Loades: *The Reign of Mary Tudor: Politics, Government and Religion in England, 1553–58* (London 1979); D. Loades: *Mary Tudor: A Life* (Oxford 1989); R. Tittler: *The Reign of Mary I* (London 1983); J. Loach and R. Tittler (eds): *The Mid-Tudor Polity c.1540–1560* (London 1980); C. Haigh (ed.): *The Reign of Elizabeth I* (London 1984).

The best recent, general surveys of Tudor government are probably provided by: D. Loades: *Tudor Government. Structures of Authority in the Sixteenth Century* (Oxford 1997); J. Guy (ed.): *The Tudor Monarchy* (London 1997).

More specialised works on specific areas of Tudor government include: for the court: D. Starkey (ed.): *The English Court from the Wars of the Roses to the Civil War* (London and New York 1987); J. Guy: *The Reign of Elizabeth I: Court and Culture in the Last Decade* (Cambridge 1995). For organs of central government: C. Coleman and D. Starkey (eds): *Revolution Reassessed. Revisions in the History of Tudor Government and Administration* (Oxford 1986); D.E. Hoak: *The King's Council in the Reign of Edward VI* (Cambridge 1976). For the law: J. Guy: *The Cardinal's Court* (Brighton 1977); J.S. Cockburn: *Crime in England 1550–1800* (London 1977); J. Pound: *Poverty and Vagrancy in Tudor England* (London 1986). For local government: J. Barry (ed.): *The Tudor and Stuart Town 1530–1688* (London and New York 1990); S. Ellis: *Tudor Frontiers and Noble Power. The Making of the British State* (Oxford 1995); S. Ellis: *Tudor Ireland. Crown, Community and the Conflict of Cultures, 1470–1603* (London and New York 1985); B. Coward: *Social Change and Continuity in Early Modern England, 1550–1750* (London and New York 1988). For Parliament: M.A.R. Graves: *The Tudor Parliaments. Crown, Lords and Commons, 1485–1603* (London and New York 1985); M.A.R. Graves: *Early Tudor Parliaments 1485–1558* (London and New York 1990); S.E. Lehmberg: *The Reformation Parliament 1529–1536* (Cambridge 1970); S.E. Lehmberg: *The Later Parliaments of Henry VIII* (Cambridge 1977); M.A.R. Graves: *Elizabethan Parliaments 1559–1601* (London and New York 1987). For the Church: C. Harper-Bill: *The Pre-Reformation Church in England* (London and New York 1996); J.A.F. Thompson: *The Early Tudor Church and Society 1485–1529* (London and New York 1993); C. Haigh: *English Reformations. Religion, Politics and Society under the Tudors* (Oxford 1993); E. Duffy: *The Stripping of the Altars. Traditional Religion in England 1400–1580* (New Haven and London 1992); F. Heal and R. O'Day (eds): *Church and Society in England: Henry VIII to James I* (London 1977). For finance: F.C. Dietz: *English Public Finance 1485–1641* (London 1964).

INDEX

Amicable Grant (1525) 131, 137
Anglican church 111–127
apprenticeship 81–2
Arthur, Prince 6, 7
Artificers, Statute of, *see* Statute of Artificers
Arundel, Henry Fitzalan, Earl of 44, 50
assize courts 54
Attainder, acts of 5, 94, 145
Augmentations, Court of 42, 47, 50, 129

Bacon, Francis 13, 142
Bedingfield, Sir Henry 44
Belknap, Edward 7
benefit of clergy 109–10, 113
Boleyn, Anne 26, 41
bonds and recognisances 5, 12–14, 112, 145
Books of Orders 82
Book of Rates 133
Booth, Charles, Bishop of Hereford 121
Brandon, Charles, Duke of Suffolk 21, 24, 73, 95, 137
Bray, Sir Reginald 7
Bryan, Francis 24, 25
Buckingham, Edward Stafford, Duke of 23–4
Burgavenny, George Lord 5, 7, 13, 15, 58
Burghley, William Cecil, Lord 21, 28–9, 30, 35, 40, 61, 69, 99, 100, 134, 135, 147–8

Calais 52, 131
Cambridge, poor relief in 81
canon law 56, 109–10
Canterbury, province of 109
Carew, Nicholas 24, 25
Carey, William 24
Catherine of Aragon 26, 114
Cecil, Robert 99, 134, 142, 147–8
Cecil, William, *see* Burghley
Chancery, Court of 55, 56, 58
Chapuys, Eustace 48
Charles V, Holy Roman Emperor 44
Chester, diocese of 116
Church, government of 109–27
Church of England, *see* Anglican Church
Clement VII, Pope 114
common law 54–71
Commission of the Peace 55
Common Pleas, Court of 54–5
Compton, Sir William 25
Council, *see* Privy Council
Council of Regency (1547) 8
Council of the Marches 74
Council of the North 74
Cranmer, Thomas Archbishop of Canterbury 18
Cromwell, Thomas 23, 39–43, 48–9, 57, 78, 96, 110, 130–3, 138, 139–40
crown lands 47, 128, 134, 135, 143
Curteys, Richard, Bishop of Chichester 117

customs and excise 47, 133, 135, 143

Dacre family 76
Darcy, Sir Thomas 10
debasement of the coinage 133, 141
Denny, Sir Anthony 22
Devereux, Robert, *see* Essex
Dissolution, Act of (1539) 138
dissolution of the monasteries (1536 and 1539) 74, 79, 96, 110, 128, 132, 138
dry stamp 10
Dublin 74–5
Dudley, Edmund 7, 10, 13, 59, 94
Dudley, John, *see* Northumberland
Dudley, Robert, *see* Leicester

Edward IV 5
Edward VI 2, 3, 4, 8–12, 16, 22, 111
Elizabeth of York 6, 113, 120
Elizabeth I 3, 4, 16, 17, 26–30, 34–7, 60–3, 97–102, 105–8, 111, 115–19, 123–7, 133–6, 141–3
Eltham, Ordinances of (1526) 25, 41, 131
Empson, Sir Richard 7, 59, 94
Enclosures 58–9, 62, 65, 74
Englefield, Sir Francis 44
'engrossing' 80
Essex, Robert Devereux, Earl of 28, 30, 61
Exchequer 42, 47, 129–30, 135
Exchequer Chamber, Court of 55
Exeter, poor relief in 81

First Fruits and Tenths, Court of 42, 47, 129
FitzHerbert's Case 99
forced loans 136
'forestalling' 80
'fruits of justice' 129

Gardiner, Stephen, Bishop of Winchester 43, 45, 46, 47, 51
Gates, Sir John 10, 22

General Surveyors, Court of 42, 129
'Gloriana' 29, 148
Great Seal 39
Gresham, Sir Thomas 141
Grey, Lady Jane 11, 16–17, 18–19, 44, 53
Grindal, Edmund, Archbishop of Canterbury 118, 119, 125
Groom of the Stool 22, 25

Hampton Court 24
Hatton, Sir Christopher 28, 30, 35
Henry VII 1, 3, 4–8, 12–14, 75–7, 84–6, 93–4, 112–13, 120
Henry VIII 2, 3, 7, 8, 16, 22–6, 31–3, 57, 78–9, 94–7, 110, 113–14, 130–3, 137–40, 141
High Commission, Court of 110
Hobart, Sir James 112
House of Commons 92, 97–102
House of Lords 92, 96, 99, 101
Hunne's Case (1514–15) 114, 121

Innocent VII, Pope 120
Ipswich, poor relief in 81
Ireland 52, 74–9, 84–8, 143
Irish parliament 75, 77

James I 135, 136
Justices of the Peace 55–6, 58, 60, 67–71, 73, 82, 89–90, 124

Kildare, Gerald, eighth Earl of 76–8, 84–8, 151
Kildare, Gerald, ninth Earl of 78, 151
King's Bench, Court of 54

Lambarde, William 60, 68
Leicester, Robert Dudley, Earl of 27, 28–9, 30, 34, 119
Legate *a latere* 113
Lichfield, diocese of 116
London, poor relief in 81
Lord Chancellor 39–40, 55, 56–60

Lord Deputy (Ireland) 74–5, 77–8
Lords Lieutenant 73
Lord Treasurer 134

Mary Stuart, Queen of Scots 27,
    98, 100
Mary Tudor 1, 2, 3, 4, 11, 16, 17,
    43–7, 51–3, 111, 115
Mildmay, Sir Walter 141
monopolies 101, 136
More, Sir Thomas 14, 102–3
Morton, John , Archbishop of
    Canterbury 39, 113

Norfolk, Thomas Howard, third
    Duke of 23–4, 95, 96
Norfolk, Thomas Howard, fourth
    Duke of 29
Northumberland, John Dudley,
    Duke of 8–12, 19, 22, 44, 53,
    146
Norton, Thomas 100
Norwich, diocese of 116
Norwich, poor relief in 81

Pace, Richard 48
Paget, William 43, 44–5, 46, 47,
    50, 51, 103
Pale, the 75, 77
Parliament 3, 46, 52, 59, 92–108
parliamentary taxation 93, 129,
    136, 137, 142–4
patronage 21, 93, 100, 118–19,
    135
Petre, Sir William 44, 51
Philip II of Spain 27, 44, 45–6
Pilgrimage of Grace (1536) 41,
    73, 103
Pole, Reginald 47, 51
Polydore Vergil 12, 23, 31, 33–4,
    57, 66, 147
poor laws 80–3
Poor Law (1563) 81, 88
Poor Law (1572) 88–9
Poor Law (1576) 89
Poor Law (1601) 89–90
Poynings, Sir Edward 77
Praemunire, statutes of 110, 112,
    132
prayer book 111

prerogative, see royal prerogative
Presence Chamber 21–2, 35
primogeniture 1
privileges, parliamentary 98–9,
    105–8
Privy Chamber 9, 17, 22, 24–5,
    27, 129
Privy Council 9, 10, 38–9, 40–1,
    43–7, 51–2, 117
'prophesyings' 118, 124
'puritan choir' 98
puritanism 118–19

quarter sessions 55–6

Raleigh, Sir Walter 27, 28
recognisances, see bonds and
    recognisances
recusancy 116–17, 143, 154
Reformation Parliament 96, 110
Renard, Simon 44, 47, 51–2,
    103
Requests, Court of 40, 55, 58
Restraint of Annates, Act in
    (1534) 114
Restraint of Appeals, Act in
    (1533) 110, 114, 122
Resumption, Act of (1515) 131
Revolt of the Northern Earls
    (1569) 61, 117, 124
Rochester, Sir Robert 44, 51
Royal Chamber 129
royal prerogative 2, 98, 105–8
royal progresses 21
royal supremacy 3–4, 56, 96, 101,
    115–19, 123–6, 138

Sadler, Sir Ralph 41, 49
Salic Law 1
sanctuary 110, 112–13
Sandys, Edwin, Bishop of
    Worcester 117; Archbishop
    of York 118
St German, Christopher 102
Secretary, 39–40, 41, 48–9
Sheffield, poor relief in 90
Sheriff, office of 73
'Silken Thomas', son of ninth Earl
    of Kildare 78
Simnel, Lambert 77, 84–5, 87

Skelton, John 24, 31, 33–4, 57, 64–5
Somerset, Edward Seymour Duke of 8–12, 145
Star Chamber, Court of 6, 39, 40, 41, 49, 55, 56–7, 58, 64–5
statute law 93, 94, 96, 97, 100, 102–5, 110, 114
Statute of Artificers (1563) 80, 81, 82
Strickland's case 99
subsidies, parliamentary 59, 93, 95, 98, 130–1, 132, 136, 142
Subsidy Act (1534) 131
Suffolk, Duke of, see Brandon, Charles
Supremacy, Act of (1534) 3, 110, 114
'surrender and regrant' 78

'tenths' and 'fifteenths' 93, 94, 143
Three Articles (1583) 125
Treason Law (1534) 3
'Tudor paternalism' 80–3
'tunnage and poundage' 94, 95, 129

Uniformity, Act of (1559) 123
Union, Act of (Wales) 74

vagrancy 62
'Vicegerent in Spirituals' 110
visitations 116, 117, 154

Wales 74, 96
Warbeck, Perkin 85, 86, 87
Wards and Liveries, Court of 42, 128, 134
wardship 128, 134
Warham, William, Archbishop of Canterbury 39, 114
Wentworth, Paul 98, 106, 107
Wentworth, Peter 98, 106, 107
Whitgift, John, Archbishop of Canterbury 110, 118, 119, 125
Winchester, William Paulet, Marquis of 44, 47, 133, 134
Wolsey, Thomas 22–6, 31–3, 38, 39, 48, 55, 56–60, 64–7, 94, 95, 113–14, 130–3, 137, 139–40
Wriothesley, Thomas, Earl of Southampton 41, 49, 139, 140
Wyatt's Rebellion (1554) 45, 46

York, diocese of 116
York, poor relief in 81
York, province of 109